criminal psychology

a beginner's guide

ray bull, claire cooke,
ruth hatcher, jessica woodhams,
charlotte bilby and tim grant

ONEWORLD

OXFORD

criminal psychology: a beginner's guide

A Oneworld Book
Published by Oneworld Publications 2006

ISBN-13: 978–1–85168–477–9
ISBN-10: 1–85168–477–8

Typeset by Jayvee, Trivandrum, India
Cover design by Two Associates
Printed and bound in Great Britain
by Biddles Ltd., Kings Lynn

Oneworld Publications
185 Banbury Road
Oxford OX2 7AR
England
www.oneworld-publications.com

criminal psychology

a beginner's guide

From anarchism to artificial intelligence and genetics to global terrorism, Beginner's Guides equip readers with the tools to fully understand the most challenging and important debates of our age. Written by experts in a clear and accessible style, books in this series are substantial enough to be thorough but compact enough to be read by anyone wanting to know more about the world they live in.

anarchism
ruth kinna

anti-capitalism
simon tormey

artificial intelligence
blay whitby

biodiversity
john spicer

bioterror & biowarfare
malcolm dando

the brain
a. al-chalabi, m.r. turner
& r.s. delamont

criminal psychology
ray bull *et al.*

democracy
david beetham

energy
vaclav smil

evolution
burton s. guttman

evolutionary psychology
robin dunbar, louise
barrett & john lycett

genetics
a. griffiths, b. guttman,
d. suzuki & t. cullis

global terrorism
leonard weinberg

NATO
jennifer medcalf

the palestine–israeli conflict
dan cohn-sherbok &
dawoud el-alami

philosophy of mind
edward feser

postmodernism
kevin hart

quantum physics
alastair i. m. rae

religion
martin forward

the small arms trade
m. schroeder, r. stohl &
d.m. smith

Forthcoming:

astrobiology
lewis dartnell

asylum
pamela goldberg

capitalism
andrew kilmister, gary
browning

cloning
aaron levine

conspiracy theories
alasdair spark

extrasolar planets
ian stevens

fair trade
jacqueline decarlo

forensic science
jay siegel

galaxies
joanne baker

human rights
david beetham

immigration
liza schuster

the irish conflict
anthony mcintyre,
david adams

mafia
james finckenauer

racism
alana lentin

radical philosophy
andrew collier

time
amarendra swarup

volcanoes
rosaly lopes

contents

preface

Criminal psychology covers a range of fascinating topics. For centuries people have been very interested in crime, and in the last hundred years psychology has grown from a fledgling discipline to one of great importance. In several countries around the world (e.g. the USA, the UK), psychology is now among the top three most popular subjects to be studied at university or college.

It is now recognized that psychology is highly relevant to many aspects of life, especially those to do with offenders, prisons, the police, witnesses, and the courts. This book has been written for members of the general public who wish to have a better understanding of criminal psychology than that which can be provided by the popular media such as newspapers and television. In this book we have explained in a reader-friendly way the research (and theory) which underpins modern criminal psychology. Thus the book will also be of interest to those commencing their studies of criminal psychology (e.g. in college or the final years of school).

We authors of the book have used everyday language to explain the many facets of criminal psychology. We have described the complexity of the issues and explained why, therefore, there are rarely simple answers or rules regarding criminal psychology (e.g. why harsh punishment may not reduce offending, that liars may not look away when deceiving you, that coercion may not produce reliable confessions).

The contents of this book would not have been possible without the help of all those people around the world who have participated in the thousands of relevant psychological studies. We would like to thank the police officers, witnesses, victims, offenders, prison officers and others who have given up their time, often in very difficult circumstances, to make a contribution. We would also like to thank Julie Blackwell-Young for her assistance with chapter eight and Aimee Jones for, among other things, collating the chapters.

Ray Bull
Leicester January 2006

criminal psychologists: within which settings do they work?

introduction

If you were asked the question 'What do criminal psychologists do in their everyday working life?', what would you answer? If you were to believe the latest television dramas you might think that the main role of criminal psychologists involves helping the police to catch criminals or engaging in the 'profiling' of offenders. If, however, you had watched films such as *The Silence of the Lambs*, then you might believe that all criminal psychologists, like Clarice Starling, attempt to gain a better insight into the minds of serious offenders by talking to convicted offenders about their crimes.

These popular conceptions of the work of criminal psychologists, while they may be true for a small number, do not represent the wide variety of roles that those trained in criminal psychology can, and do, work. From assisting the police in investigations, providing advice on interviewing of suspects or witnesses, working as expert witnesses in court cases, working in the rehabilitation of offenders, conducting criminal psychology research or working in academia, the work of criminal psychologists is varied and wide reaching.

This chapter aims to present a balanced view of the profession of criminal psychology and to introduce the reader to the variety of roles within which criminal psychologists can, and do, work. It will guide you through the criminal justice process and provide a brief overview of how criminal psychologists may contribute their expertise at each stage. Further and more in-depth information can be found in the following chapters.

what is criminal/forensic psychology?

The term 'criminal psychology' has been defined in a number of different ways. Even today there is no accepted definition. For example, ten years ago two leading criminal psychologists in the UK defined it as 'that branch of applied psychology which is concerned with the collection, examination and presentation of evidence for judicial purposes' (Gudjonsson and Haward 1998, p. 1). It would seem from this explanation that criminal psychology is concerned with investigative (those to do with the police) and court processes. However, with the growth in the last quarter of a century in the involvement of criminal psychologists in the assessment and treatment of offenders following their sentencing, it would not be surprising if there were some disagreement with a definition which would exclude these groups of professionals from being called criminal psychologists.

It would seem therefore that a wider definition of the term is needed. A leading American psychologist has gone some way to provide this. He described criminal psychology as 'any application of psychological knowledge or methods to a task faced by the legal system' (Wrightsman 2001, p. 2). This more inclusive definition involves the whole of the legal system. As you will see in the coming pages, criminal psychologists can be involved in all areas of the judicial process (including post sentence) and a broad-based definition is needed to encompass all of this work.

In 1981 Professor Lionel Haward, one of the UK's founding fathers of criminal psychology, described the four roles that psychologists may perform when they become professionally involved in criminal proceedings. These are:

1. *Clinical*: in this situation the psychologist will usually be involved in the assessment of an individual in order to provide a clinical judgement. The psychologist could use interviews, assessment tools or psychometric tests (i.e. special question-naires) to aid in his or her assessment. These assessments can inform the police, the courts, or the prison and probation ser-vices about the psychological functioning of an individual and can therefore influence how the different sections of the crim-inal justice system process the individual in question. For example, a psychologist may be asked to assess individuals in order to determine whether they are fit to stand trial or whether they have a mental illness which means that they would not understand the proceedings.

2. *Experimental*: this can involve the psychologist performing research in order to inform a case. This can involve carrying out experimental tests in order to illustrate a point or provide further information to the courts (for example, how likely it is that someone can correctly identify an object in the hand of an individual from a distance of 100 metres at twilight). Alternatively, it can involve psychologists providing the court with a summary of current research findings which may be relevant to the case in question.

3. *Actuarial*: in this instance the word 'actuarial' relates to the use of statistics in order to inform a case. One example of how a psychologist may act in an actuarial role is if they are required to present actuarial information relating to the probability of an event occurring to the court. For example, a court may wish to know how likely an offender is to reoffend before the sentence is decided. In such a case, a psychologist could be called upon in order to inform the pre-sentence report to the court.

4. *Advisory*: in this role the psychologist may provide advice to the police about how to proceed with an investigation. For example, an offender's profile could inform the investigation, or

advice could be provided about how best to interview a particular suspect. Alternatively, a prosecution or defence lawyer may ask for advice on how best to cross-examine a vulnerable witness or another expert witness. This role involves the use of the psychologist's expertise in order to advise the police, courts or prison and probation services.

As you can see, psychologists can be used in a variety of different scenarios within the criminal justice system and for a number of different reasons. The next few sections will examine in more detail how psychologists can and do contribute their expertise to aid the work of the criminal justice system. This list of roles, however, does not claim to be exhaustive – there are many more ways in which psychologists play their part. We have therefore chosen the most well-known roles in order to give an indication of what working in criminal psychology can involve.

criminal investigations

The role of a psychologist in criminal investigations can take a variety of forms. Professor Laurence Alison of the University of Liverpool has suggested a number of ways in which the expertise of a psychologist could aid the police and support the work that they do.

> It is important to appreciate that the ways in which psychologists can contribute extends well beyond the process of profiling offenders. Indeed the apprehension of the offender would be assisted by enhancing police decision-making and leadership skills, improving methods of interviewing witnesses and victims, developing accurate methods of recording, collating and analysing data on preconvictions of offenders, developing suspect prioritization systems based on empirical research and enhancing intelligence-led policing and the use of informants.

(Alison 2005)

From the list contained within this quote, it can be seen that the role of the psychologist in assisting the police can be wide-ranging. The next sections will focus on some of these roles in more detail.

crime analysis

Crime analysis (sometimes also called intelligence analysis) is one field of work which draws upon criminal psychological methods. Crime analysts are generally employed by the police (or policing agencies, for example in the UK the National Crime and Operations Faculty and the National Crime Squad) in order to analyse crime data to aid the police carry out their roles.

One of the most common roles of crime analysts is that of case linkage. This process involves the linkage of crimes based on the similarities in the behaviours of the offender as reported by the victim or as inferred from the crime scene. For example, let us examine a rape case committed by a stranger on a woman walking home alone after a night out with her friends. Crime analysts could use the details of this case – the fact that she had just left a nightclub, that the rapist took some of her clothing away from the scene with him, and the content of the threats used towards the woman – in order to check against an already established database of similar crimes to see whether there are any similarities to past crimes. If matches are found – the same threats were used, similar items of clothing taken by a rapist, and it was in a close geographical location to another rape – then this information can be used by the police to investigate the potential that the same individual offender has committed both crimes. This allows the focusing of the resources of the investigation in order to avoid duplication of work. (The case linkage work that crime analysts carry out, along with a case study of case linkage in relation to Jack the Ripper, is outlined in much more detail in chapter 2).

CASE STUDY

Sarah is a criminal psychologist who is employed by a national police agency within the UK. Sarah has received information from a local police force on a serious undetected stranger rape. She will read through the statements and reports relating to the case and pick out information relating to the behaviour of the perpretator. This will then be compared to the behavioural indicators recorded from similar crimes, to look for any indications that the same person committed more than one crime.

Sarah will then prepare a report for the police, summarising as to whether the behavioural evidence indicates that the undetected crime was likely to have been committed by the same individual as any of the crimes held on the national database. This information can be used by the police force to focus their investigation, or if the crime on the database is solved, the police can use Sarah's report to aid them when building a case to arrest this individual for the undetected rape.

offender profiling or criminal investigative analysis

Offender profiling has received a great deal of attention from the media in recent years. Media reporting of the utilization of criminal psychologists in high profile cases has introduced the general public to the notion of offender profiling. While this has raised the profile of the field, it could be argued that the (largely) sensationalist portrayal of profiling has resulted in a general confusion of what profiling actually is, how often it is done and who does it. This uncertainty amongst the general public is not altogether surprising however, as there is an absence of an agreed definition of the term 'profiling', even in academic circles.

What we can be clear about is that profiling uses information gleaned from the crime scene relating to the offender's behaviour during the crime. This can be pooled with other information, such as victim statements (if available), in order to draw conclusions about the nature of the person who committed the crime. Was the crime planned meticulously or was it impulsive? Does the offender live locally to the crime scene? What age range is the offender likely to fall into? What gender is the offender? This information can then be used to aid the police in investigations and in targeting resources.

But how exactly is a profiler able to look at the scene and use this to specify the characteristics of the offender? The answer to this question is not entirely clear mainly because different people involved in offender profiling can, and do, use a variety of techniques in order to reach their conclusions. Even those individuals who claim to be working from the same theoretical standpoint can still vary in how the theory is applied to any given case. Chapter 2 describes the different approaches of clinical and statistical profiling in detail.

interviewing, detecting deception and eyewitness research

One of the most important tasks during an investigation is collecting reliable evidence in order to put together a case of what happened during the event in question. One of the main sources of this evidence is the people who were eyewitnesses to the event. In order to gain this information, an interview needs to be conducted by the investigating police officers with the aim of gaining as much accurate information from the witness as possible. In addition, once a suspect has been identified, he or she too is interviewed in order to gain his or her view of events and to possibly extract a confession to the crime. Hence the interview (whether with a witness or suspect) and the manner in which it is conducted can be crucial to a case.

It is not surprising, therefore, when you think of the processes (those relating to memory and the retrieval of memory) that are involved in the interview situation, that psychologists have been interested in this area for years. Given research findings such as those that state that the recall of events by witnesses can be manipulated by the interviewer (either intentionally or unintentionally – for example, by the type of questions asked), it is clear that those carrying out the interviews need to receive training in how to conduct the interviews appropriately. Psychologists have been instrumental in developing guidance and advice on how best to interview witnesses and suspects and have also provided training to various police forces on these techniques. (For more on this see chapter 4).

The police can also use psychologists in order to gain advice on how to interview particular types of witnesses or suspects. For example, psychologists have conducted research into interviews with vulnerable witnesses such as the young, the elderly and learning disabled witnesses. This research can be used to inform the police on how best to retrieve the information that they require

CASE STUDY

Robert is an academic who works within the field of criminal psychology. He specialises in the interviewing of vulnerable witnesses, such as the elderly and the young, and has been carrying out active research within this area for a number of years. The police have asked him to provide them with some advice in relation to a case they are working on.

An adult male has been found murdered and the only known witness is a little boy. The police wish to gain as much accurate information from the child as possible in order to help their case but are unsure as to how much they can rely on his statement due to his age and the trauma he has been through. The police also need advice on how best to approach the little boy so as not to traumatise him any further. They therefore need the help of an expert in this area and contact Robert, who is able to use the findings from his research to advise the police.

from such witnesses without causing them too much stress while at the same time ensuring that the information received is as accurate as possible.

Research performed by criminal psychologists investigating the detection of deception also has useful applications for the police when interviewing witnesses and in particular suspects. How do people behave when they are lying and what cues can police officers look out for that might indicate that the suspects are lying about their whereabouts during the crime? Is it possible to tell with a level of accuracy when someone is lying? And are polygraphs reliable in detecting deception? These questions will be discussed in more detail in chapter 5.

police psychology

The information in this section has, thus far, been concerned with the application of psychological knowledge to assist in police investigation. However, there is another field within which the work of psychologists, and the application of their knowledge, is useful to the police. Like many organizations, the police force itself presents its own challenges – what type of person makes a good police officer? What is the best way to train police officers? How might the attendance at unpleasant scenes of crime, or repeated exposure to negative events, impact on an individual and how are those affected in this way best treated?

This area of work is not a new one – psychologists, both occupational and criminal, have been advising the police on such matters for the last twenty-five years or so. Psychologists have contributed their knowledge to the process of police officer recruitment through the introduction of psychometric tests which measure psychological characteristics that may be important in relation to such work. These could assess, for example, whether a person is an assertive individual, open to persuasion, and conscious of detail. Psychologists have also provided advice on the composition of interviews and assessment centres which will eliminate those who do not have the necessary qualities for the role as well as providing an indication of those who will prosper in such a role.

Another important area of police interest where psychologists have an ongoing input is the moderation of police stress. The stress faced by police officers is somewhat different from that in other types of employment. Whereas stress can be elevated in most jobs through organizational change, such as decreased workload or a pay rise, the police can be faced with unexpected, perhaps threatening, situations at any time during their daily work. These events, due to their unpredictable nature, cannot necessarily be mediated by organizational change so the police also need stress management measures that can assist at an individual level, as and when they are needed. Psychologists have been instrumental in advising the police on what mechanisms would be beneficial (such as peer counselling and self-help programmes), but will also provide professional services to police officers who require more intensive stress management.

expert witnesses

Court cases can involve complex issues including the presentation of information that is judged to be beyond the knowledge of the average layperson who may sit on a jury. In such situations, the court permits the calling of an expert witness who, by definition, has an expertise relating to the issue in question. Under these circumstances expert witnesses are permitted to provide their opinion (rather than the facts) on the issue being discussed. The way that expert witnesses are called to the court, however, varies from one jurisdiction to another. For example, in some countries within Europe, an expert witness is called by the court itself in order to provide information as and when it is needed. However, in the UK and USA, the expert is instructed by either the defence or prosecution in order to provide extra strength to their version of events.

The use of the psychologist as an expert witness has, in the past, been constricted by the notion of the expert having to provide information that is beyond the knowledge of the average person. Historically then, the admissibility of a psychologist's opinion was often limited to providing evidence relating to mental impairment or the psychological functioning of an individual. However, in recent years, the psychologists' expertise has been increasingly recognized and can now be called upon as evidence in relation to a wide variety of issues. Some examples of these are the impact of interviewing techniques on a suspect or witness, the reliability of eyewitness testimony, the clinical assessment of a suspect or witness, or the use of profiling techniques during an investigation.

criminal psychologists and assessment and treatment of offenders

Criminal psychologists, especially within Australia, Canada and the UK, are heavily involved in work concerning the assessment, rehabilitation and management of offenders, either in the community or when held in incarceration. This role can involve working with the offenders to reduce their likelihood of reoffending in the future or a more clinical role addressing the psychological needs of offenders. These psychological needs may (or may not) result from the effects of crime they committed (for example, the development of post-traumatic stress disorder or realization of the impact of their offence on their victim) or the environment within which they are held (for example, developing depression due to being away from the family or anxiety brought on by repetitive bullying from other prisoners). This work can be both varied and challenging in nature.

One of the first and ongoing concerns of a criminal psychologist working with offenders post-sentence is the assessment of the offenders. This encompasses an in-depth analysis of their risk of reoffending, their risk of harm (to others as well as themselves) and their needs (such as accommodation, finances and mental

CASE STUDY

Claire is a criminal psychologist who is employed to work with offenders within prison environment. She is currently organising an offending behaviour programme for twelve convicted offenders which will address why they committed crimes and what measures can be put in place to prevent further offending on their release from prison. She is responsible for assessing offenders to ensure their suitability for the programme and so carries out a number of interviews and assessments with each potential programme attendee. For the duration of the programme she will spend four hours a week with her co-facilitator working through the programme exercises and will prepare reports detailing the progress of each offender through the programme.

Claire is also responsible for one-to-one work with offenders who have a tendency to carry out self-harm behaviours and those who are at risk of attempting suicide. She will meet with these on a regular basis in order to monitor their psychological state.

health, for example). These assessments can be used in the management of the offenders' highlighted risk and needs, informing the planning of the activities that the offenders will undertake during their sentence. This could include the provision of basic skills courses, treatment programmes, one to one work on particular issues, and so on. In addition, if an offender is on a community sentence and has been assessed to be a high risk to the public, then it may be the case that the offender becomes subject to monitoring arrangements in order to reduce the risk that he or she poses. Psychologists can provide an input to each of these arrangements on an operational level but can also provide managerial and advisory support to those delivering such interventions.

Over recent years there has been a growth in the use of treatment programmes with offenders (see chapter 10 for more detailed information). Criminal psychologists have been active in this development contributing to the design, delivery and management of programmes which attempt to address the offenders' thoughts, attitudes and behaviours that contribute to their offending behaviour, and prevent further offending. Psychologists are also involved in the management of these programmes, ensuring that the right offenders are placed on such programmes and that the programmes are delivered in the manner in which the designer intended. Research has shown that badly delivered programmes can at best be ineffective but at worst be damaging.

However, the role of the prison or probation psychologist is not limited to rehabilitation related work. Criminal psychologists within these settings can also be involved in undertaking research, overseeing training of prison or probation staff, preparing reports for the courts detailing the risk level, needs and other information relating to the individual offender, attending court, attending team and area meetings and the inevitable administration!

criminal psychologists and academia/research

With the growth of interest in criminal psychology over recent years, there has been an increased demand for courses which teach the theory and practice of criminal psychology. With the inevitable growth in criminal psychology courses, there has been a corresponding increase in the number of criminal psychologists working within academia.

So what do those people actually do? Well, the obvious answer is that they teach students about criminal psychology: about the psychology of criminal behaviour, of the courtroom, psychology and investigation, the assessment and treatment of offenders and also about how to carry out criminal psychological research. This teaching can be at undergraduate or postgraduate level and can be delivered in a variety of different ways.

However, the role of the academic criminal psychologist is not only limited to teaching. The other main role of academics is to carry out research within their field of interest. Most academics have their own research interests that develop over time and they

CASE STUDY

John trained in the field of criminal psychology a number of years ago, completing a postgraduate qualification and working as a criminal psychologist within the secure estate for five years. However, he has always been interested in disseminating knowledge to others and so recently made the decision to move into academia. He is now responsible for delivering academic courses in criminal psychology to individuals who have already studied at undergraduate level and wish to go on to work within this field.

John is also very interested in offenders with severe learning disabilities and their understanding of their crimes. He and a colleague have just secured funding to carry out some research investigating this notion. They plan to hire a researcher to work with them on this project and will publish their findings once the work is complete. He hopes that this research will inform not only those working with learning-disabled offenders but also court decisions in relation to how these individuals are processed and sentenced. It is also possible that at some point in the future he may become an expert witness in a case where a defendant is severely learning disabled. He could be asked to testify as to whether, in his professional opinion, the defendant had the intention to commit an offence.

are usually encouraged by their employers to expand their knowledge of these specialisms by researching them further. The ability to do this can often be dependent on a variety of outside forces, however, such as the availability of funding and access to privileged data or to imprisoned individuals. From a personal point of view, while at times this work can be frustrating, tedious and time-consuming, it is also very interesting and hugely rewarding. Most criminal psychologists who work in universities also are required to be involved in professional practice such as giving advice in some of the many ways outlined in this chapter.

conclusions

We have tried to present a definition of criminal psychology along with information about how various criminal psychologists may work, what roles they may perform and what institutions may employ them for this work.

The work of the psychologist within the criminal justice system can certainly take many routes depending on the specialism of the particular psychologist. From aiding the police in their investigations, advising in the selection of police officers, providing expert evidence to the court, working with offenders conducting assessments and interventions, carrying out research or imparting their own knowledge to future criminal psychologists, the work is varied and challenging.

Criminal psychology will continue to develop and psychologists are likely to become even more involved in the varied facets of crime and the criminal justice process. There is certainly much more to investigate and learn about how criminal psychologists could contribute to the understanding of crime and how they can aid the workings of justice systems. The remaining chapters of this book will look at current aspects of criminal psychology and provide information about the latest issues and developments within the various fields.

recommended further reading

Ainsworth, P. B. (2000) *Psychology and crime: Myths and reality.* Harlow, Essex: Longman.

Alison, L. (2005) *The Forensic Psychologist's casebook: psychological profiling and criminal investigation.* Cullompton, UK: Willan.

Carson, D. and Bull, R. (2003) *Handbook of psychology in legal contexts*, 2nd edn. Chichester: Wiley.

Gudjonsson, G. H. and Haward, L. R. C. (1998) *Forensic psychology: A guide to practice.* London: Routledge.

Hollin, C. R. (ed.) (2003) *The essential handbook of offender assessment and treatment.* Chichester: John Wiley.

Howitt, D. (2006) What is forensic and criminal psychology? In D. Howitt *Forensic and criminal psychology*, 2nd edn, pp. 1–16. Harlow, Essex: Pearson, Prentice-Hall.

Wrightsman, L. S. (2001) *Forensic psychology.* Bekmont, CA: Wadsworth.

online resources

http://www.bps.org.uk
This is the web site of the British Psychological Society which will contain up to date information on how to become a criminal or forensic psychologist.

offender profiling and linking crime

The term 'offender profiling' is one with which most of us are familiar. Its recent appearances in the media have certainly raised the profile of criminal psychology and a number of students are keen to work in this area. Unfortunately, the media portrayal of offender profiling has often been far from accurate. As a result of its general popularity, much has been written on this topic and a comprehensive review of the literature is beyond the scope of this chapter: rather we aim to give you a more accurate introduction to the topic of offender profiling. It will also introduce you to the equally fascinating but relatively unpublicized practice of linking crimes, which has at times been considered a type of offender profiling. However, the aims of the two processes are quite different and therefore they are discussed separately within this chapter.

offender profiling

Offender profiling is the inferring of an offender's characteristics from his or her crime scene behaviour. For example, a profiler might try to infer a criminal's age, gender or employment history from the way he or she has behaved during a crime. This practice has been referred to by other names including criminal profiling, psychological profiling and specific profile analysis. Offender profiling is typically used with crimes where the offender's identity is unknown and with serious types of crime, such as murder or rape. Profilers are also likely to work on crime *series*, which are collections of crimes that are thought to have been committed by the same offender.

The different types of offender profiling can be broken down broadly into two types: geographical profiling and the profiling of an offender's personal characteristics. The latter is what people most commonly associate with the term offender profiling.

The types of tasks that offender profilers might be asked to complete depend on the type of profiler they are. A geographical profiler could be asked to identify the likely location of an offender's home from the geography of his or her known offences. An offender profiler might be asked to construct a profile of an unknown offender giving details of his or her likely characteristics as inferred from the offender's behaviour at the crime scene. When an offender is apprehended the profiler might also be asked to advise the police on the way that particular suspects should be interviewed. As you can see, offender profiling is therefore an umbrella term for a number of different practices.

Having identified what offender profiling is, we should address the question 'Who are offender profilers?' In 1995, Gary Copson investigated this issue and found that the majority of profilers in Britain were typically academic or criminal psychologists. Psychiatrists, police officers and police civilian staff were also represented within his sample of offender profilers: clearly offender profilers are themselves a varied group of people.

It may come as a surprise to learn that offender profiling is rarely a full-time occupation. While the media tend to portray offender profiling as a job in itself, very few individuals, within the United Kingdom at least, conduct offender profiling full-time. Most offender profilers are called in as consultants: the role is not as widely practised as the media portray. For example, Copson's study found only seventy-five instances of offender profilers giving advice in 1994, and this was the highest number recorded in one year for the time span of his study.

A number of different materials can be used by an offender profiler in constructing a profile or in geographically profiling an offender's likely home. One of the most important sources of information for constructing a profile would be the victims' or witnesses' accounts of the crime. In some types of crime it is possible that a victim's account may not be available, for example in the case of murder. In such cases, an offender profiler might instead have to rely on post-mortem reports, sketches of the crime scene and accounts from others about the victim. Regardless of the documentation used in constructing the profile, an offender profiler has a lot of information to absorb and process when trying to profile the offenders or their location.

geographical profiling

Geographical profiling is typically used to identify the likely area of an offender's residence from the location of the crime. Such an approach can be very useful in narrowing down a pool of suspects or enabling the police to prioritize an area for investigation or DNA sampling.

Geographical profiling has its history in environmental criminology. The aim of environmental criminologists was to identify areas where criminals were likely to offend from the locations of the offenders' residences: the aim of geographical profiling is the reverse. Using the locations of an offender's crimes as his or her starting point, the geographical profiler tries to predict the area in which the offender lives.

Although the aims of the two disciplines are different, they are based on the same theories. One of these is the principle of distance decay. This is based on the notion that when people are looking for something, they will only travel as far as they have to: as the distance between them and their target object increases, they are therefore less likely to travel to obtain it. Applying this to crime, if offenders have to choose between two different targets, if all other factors are equal, they will choose the one that is geographically closer to them.

Another criminological principle that is used in geographical profiling is the rational choice theory which predicts that offenders will often engage in a cost–benefit analysis when deciding where to offend. When deciding whether to travel to obtain a target object, the criminals will weigh up the costs (e.g. the effort of travel), with the benefits (e.g. how much they desire the object). A commercial robber might therefore be prepared to travel further to commit a robbery with higher financial rewards. A rapist whose sexual fantasies relate to a particular type of victim might be prepared to travel further to seek out such a victim.

Within geographical profiling there is also the idea of a buffer zone which relates to both of the above principles. This is a zone located around an offender's home where he or she will not offend because, while the effort of travel is minimal, the likelihood of being recognized and therefore apprehended is higher. The benefits of minimal travel are therefore outweighed by the potential of being caught.

Routine Activities Theory and Pattern Theory are also relevant to geographical profiling. These suggest that criminals will offend in an area with which they are familiar. In other words, while criminals are going about their daily life, they will notice potential targets. A burglar might therefore notice that a family are going on holiday and target this house in their absence. The area with which criminals are familiar and which surrounds their residence has been called the 'home range', while the area in which they commit crimes has been called the 'criminal range'.

These theories also relate to the idea in geographical profiling that offenders have a cognitive or mental map of their (familiar) geographical areas. Like offenders, we also have mental maps of the areas with which we are familiar. The distances between places in our cognitive maps are unlikely to reflect real distances: instead perceived distance plays an important role. For example, if we are familiar with a place that is easy to get to because of good transport links, we tend to perceive it as closer than it actually is. Offenders are no different. For example, the transport available to burglars has been found to affect the distance they travelled to commit burglaries. Those with cars tended to travel further than those who were on foot. By travelling in a car, the journey takes less time and thus the distance to a property seems less.

These theories have led to the development in criminal psychology of geographical profiling principles and definitions of types (i.e. typologies) of offenders. Two researchers have been largely responsible for these developments: Dr Kim Rossmo and Professor David Canter. Both have developed typologies of offenders which have some similarities. Rather than describing these in detail, it suffices to say that a distinction exists within both sets of typologies between two types of offender that affects the likely success of geographical profiling.

A distinction is drawn between offenders termed marauders (or hunters) and commuters (or poachers). The marauders are hypothesized to move outwards from their residence to offend. Each time they go out to offend, the direction in which they travel can change and these changes in direction can reflect where the offenders have previously committed crimes. Rather than return to the same area, which could be risky, the offenders might travel outwards in a different direction. The marauder's home range and criminal range therefore overlap.

In contrast to marauders, commuters travel away from their home to a specific area where they offend. This could be because the commuters are in search of a particular type of victim/target that cannot be obtained within their home range, and their criminal range is therefore unlikely to overlap with their home range.

Research with stranger rapists (rapists that attack victims previously unknown to them) and serial arsonists has confirmed that for these types of criminals, the marauder pattern of offending is more common, whereas the pattern for serial burglars is less clear. However, research has suggested that offenders may change their geographical pattern of offending, sometimes behaving as marauders and at other times behaving as commuters. One study examined a serial rapist who offended in Italy over a considerable number of years and it revealed that the offender sometimes behaved as a marauder but at other times as a commuter. Clearly it would be unwise to assume that offenders fit one typology or another.

Geographical profiling principles have been developed in England for the marauder type of offender by Professor David Canter and colleagues. These are based on the Circle Theory of Environmental Range which predicts that all things being equal, the shape of an offender's criminal and home range will be circular, with the home itself being located in the centre of the circle. When the home location is unknown, which is the case for geographical profilers, its approximate location can be predicted by drawing a circle through the two most geographically distant offences. The offender's home should therefore be located within the circle and also towards the centre of the circle. This is because the two most geographically distant offences will also be those furthest from the offender's home. This model has been applied to serial rape, arson and burglary with some success.

As well as relying on statistical approaches for geographical profiling, geographical profilers also consider issues such as the offender's likely motivation for the offences and the characteristics of the physical environment in which his or her offending takes place. Such factors could skew an offender's journey to crime and therefore affect the appropriateness of statistical models.

The effectiveness of geographical profiling has not received a great deal of attention, though there are some reports regarding its accuracy. For example, between 1991 and 2001 Rossmo's geographical profiling system, *Rigel*, was used in the investigation of 1,426 crimes. Its effectiveness was assessed by comparing the size of the total area over which the offences occurred to the (smaller) size of area beginning to be searched on the basis of the geographical profile. On average, the offender's residence was correctly identified having searched approximately just the central five per cent of the offence area. Its effectiveness seemed to vary depending on the type of crime, with it being most effective for arson.

profiling personal characteristics

The profiling of someone's personal characteristics is more commonly associated with offender profiling and is the practice most often portrayed in the media. The types of characteristics profiled (as shown in the media and in published reports of profiling) include demographic characteristics such as an offender's gender, age, ethnicity, educational and employment history. This approach assumes that the way a crime is committed is related to the characteristics of the person, which enables the profiler to draw inferences about the characteristics of a criminal from the way in which he or she behaved during the crime.

The different approaches to this type of profiling can be broadly broken down into three categories. The first is what is known as *statistical profiling*. This approach aims to generate statistical relationships between actions displayed at crime scenes and offender characteristics and is carried out through the use of large-scale databases of solved crimes. For example, such researchers might find that 85 per cent of rapists that use a condom during a rape (e.g. to avoid leaving semen to be DNA tested) have previously had contact with law enforcement for their sexual offending, be that a conviction or just being arrested. When such a relationship has been established and validated, the statistical profiler can analyse the circumstances of an offence and, using these statistical relationships, can make probabilistic inferences about the likely characteristics of the offender responsible.

An alternative approach is *clinical profiling*. Clinical profilers, rather than using databases of offences, develop their inferences about an offender's characteristics from their clinical experience of working with apprehended offenders. They are therefore acting in a similar way to statistical profilers, but their inferences are based on their own personal experience and, of course, rely on their accurate recollection of these. This approach to profiling has been criticized by advocates of statistical profiling. They argue that the profiles produced by clinical profilers could vary as a result of the individual nature of each clinical profiler's experience.

Another approach to profiling is that of the Federal Bureau of Investigation (FBI) in the United States. On the basis of interviews with serial offenders, FBI profilers have developed typologies of offenders that are thought to differ in their offending behaviour and therefore in their characteristics. One such example is the distinction made between *disorganized* and *organized* murderers, and another, the four typologies of rapist: *power reassurance, anger retaliation, power assertive* and *anger excitation*. This approach has continued to develop with time, but other profilers have criticized the empirical basis of this approach because of the small number of offenders on which the typologies were initially developed. Also this approach relies on the accounts of apprehended offenders for the development of inferences. It is quite possible that apprehended offenders differ in the way they commit their offences from offenders who remain at large. It would be extremely hard to address this criticism due to the ethical difficulties and practicalities surrounding interviewing unapprehended offenders about their criminal histories.

Having considered this criticism, we now move on to consider the assumptions underlying the profiling of personal characteristics from crime scene behaviour.

the assumptions of offender profiling

When profiling the characteristics of a person, the profiler is assuming that the behaviours shown at the crime scene are a result of the person's characteristics rather than determined by the situation. It is quite clear that this cannot be entirely the case: in some types of crime the involvement of another person, such as the victim, will mean that the offender will also to an extent be reacting to this person's behaviour. However, to successfully profile personal characteristics from crime scene behaviour there would have to be some elements of the crime scene behaviour that are more indicative of the person than of the situation. One task for researchers of offender profiling is to determine which behaviours these are.

There must therefore be stable relationships between characteristics and behaviour for profiling to work. Typically, the types of characteristics described in an offender profile are demographic. In such situations the profiler is therefore assuming a relationship between behaviour and demographic characteristics. Some researchers have queried whether an offender's demographic characteristics would influence their behaviour and have questioned their inclusion in offender profiles. Instead, as suggested by personality psychologists, it is more likely that a person's thoughts, goals, emotions and past experiences will affect their behaviour in a situation. Offender profiles that infer how a criminal will perceive situations or infer his or her likely past experiences might therefore be more valid than those inferring demographic characteristics. However, it is questionable how useful such information would be to the police.

An offender profiler making inferences from crime scene behaviour as to how the offender might behave in their daily lives is assuming the existence of stable relationships between characteristics and behaviour. Assuming a degree of behavioural consistency across situations is termed 'cross-situational consistency'.

If it is being assumed that offenders' characteristics will influence the way they behave during a crime, then it follows that this should be the case across all their crimes. In other words offenders will, to some extent, be consistent in the way they behave across crimes of the same type. Professor Canter called this the 'offender consistency hypothesis' which has its roots in personality psychology. Consistency across crimes is a special case of cross-situational consistency.

In addition to assuming consistency across crimes, if it is believed that certain crime scene behaviours are related to certain offender characteristics, then it follows that offenders displaying similar crime scene behaviours should have similar characteristics. This has been termed the 'homology assumption'.

Researchers from personality psychology have spent a great deal of time investigating the validity of some of these assumptions and criminal psychologists have also begun to test them empirically. Their findings are reported in the next section.

empirical evidence for the theoretical assumptions of offender profiling

As noted above, there are three assumptions that underlie the practice of offender profiling. Some have been adapted from personality psychology, others relate directly to this particular criminal psychology practice. These are now explained in turn and the evidence supporting their validity outlined.

cross-situational consistency

The study of behavioural consistency, including cross-situational consistency, has been a focus for personality and social psychologists for decades. However, none of this previous research on cross-situational consistency considered criminal behaviour.

Whether offenders show similarity between the way they behave during their crimes and the way they behave in non-criminal situations is a question that has yet to be researched in criminal psychology. However, some studies in the personality psychology literature seem promising. Some recent research has found that the more psychologically similar the situations being compared, the greater the behavioural consistency observed. This has been demonstrated with aggressive behaviour, which could be considered closer to criminal behaviour than other types of behaviour psychologists have investigated.

Researchers of personality psychology have explained that psychological similarity relates to what a situation means to us and what feelings, thoughts, expectations or goals it triggers. The psychological similarity of situations is increasingly recognized as an important factor in determining the likely degree of behavioural consistency. However, how someone interprets a situation is likely to be quite idiosyncratic, depending on their own cognitive abilities and past experiences. (You might be able to think of a situation where you have interpreted someone's behaviour in a way which was different from a friend's interpretation.)

the offender consistency hypothesis

The assumption of consistency across crimes appears to be faring well. This may be because an offender's crimes represent psychologically similar situations. Psychologists studying non-criminal behaviour have suggested that some types of behaviour show more consistency than others. Essentially, research has suggested that behaviour generated by the individual shows greater consistency than behaviour elicited by the environment. The former is viewed as self-generated, reflecting personal goals and desires, and involves acting on the environment. Such behaviours are therefore hypothesized as relating to the psychology of the individual.

From these findings, it seems quite logical to hypothesize that criminal behaviour, which could be considered need- or desire-driven, would show consistency. It could also be hypothesized that more interpersonal types of crime would show less consistency, because the additional environmental stimulus of victims or witnesses introduces more potential for variability.

Criminal psychologists have only recently started to investigate whether criminals are consistent in their offending behaviour. The types of crime that have been investigated include arson, stranger sexual assaults, commercial and residential burglary, commercial robbery and murder. Although the number of studies conducted is small and hence the findings are far from conclusive, so far the research supports the assumption that offenders show a degree of consistency in their offending behaviour. As with research into non-criminal populations, what is also evident is that consistency varies depending on the type of behaviour being observed. In the studies conducted so far, behaviours relating to distance travelled to commit crimes and controlling the victim show the greatest consistency.

the homology assumption

The question of whether offenders who behave in a similar manner during their crimes also share similar demographic characteristics has been examined using a sample of stranger rapists, but the study found no evidence to support this.

Having now considered the three assumptions that underpin the practice of offender profiling, it is clearly of concern that thus far it is only the offender consistency hypothesis that shows evidence of sound empirical support. Despite this, much more research would need to be conducted before concluding that the theoretical basis for offender profiling is unsound. In the next section we move on from the assumptions of offender profiling to consider the research that has evaluated the actual practice of offender profiling.

evaluations of offender profiling in practice

In the published literature and on the Internet it is easy to find case studies of successful applications of offender profiling to real criminal investigations. At face value this is indeed good news. However, when reading such reports it is important to remember that the successful cases are those most likely to be publicized. While it is very positive that profiling has been successful in specific cases it is important for the acceptance of profiling as a scientific practice that its effectiveness is demonstrated through empirical research.

Some empirical evaluations of offender profiling have been conducted and these will be briefly mentioned here. Two studies attempted to profile stranger rapists' criminal histories from their crime scene behaviour and both reported some limited success. A study that tried to predict the characteristics of burglars from their crime scene behaviour also achieved some success in predicting characteristics such as offender demographics (e.g. age) and previous criminal history. These studies have searched for relationships between offender characteristics and actions at the behavioural level. Other recent studies have investigated such relationships at a thematic level: themes that describe the actual behaviours, for example, pseudo-intimate behaviours, are developed. Unfortunately, the findings are modest with a few associations being found between behavioural themes and previous criminal histories. It is possible that stronger associations between characteristics and behaviour would be found were more personality-related factors investigated.

As well as actually testing whether profiling is possible, some researchers have conducted consumer satisfaction surveys, asking the users of offender profiles to rate their usefulness. In Britain, Gary Copson found that over seventy-five per cent of the police officers questioned found the profilers' advice useful. This was mainly, they said, because it increased their understanding of the offender or supported their perceptions of the offence/offender. However, only three per cent said the advice had helped identify the actual offender. (Fifty-seven per cent of the cases had been solved.) Most of the police officers did say that they would seek the advice of a profiler again.

A similar study was conducted in the Netherlands, where only six profiles existed which could be assessed. In contrast to the British study, the feedback from the police officers was negative. Most complained that the advice in the profile was too general or was not practical given the resources the officers had available to them. Some indicated that the profiler's advice was ignored because it did not match their own opinions. These findings cannot be given too much weight, however, since they are based on a very small sample of officers.

As well as measuring satisfaction, the British study assessed the accuracy of the profilers' advice. This was done with a sub-sample of cases since only fifty-seven per cent had been solved. The comments made by the profiler were assessed against what was known about the apprehended offender. Of the comments made in these profiles, only a third could be verified. On average, approximately two comments were correct for every comment that was incorrect. Clinical profilers were more accurate than statistical profilers with seventy-nine per cent of their verifiable comments being correct. On the face of things this seems very positive, but this figure also means that twenty-one per cent of the advice given was incorrect and could have potentially misled an investigation.

case linkage

In this section we consider a less publicized way in which criminal psychology can aid police investigations – case linkage. Case linkage refers to the identification of offences believed to be committed by the same offender based on their behavioural similarity. This practice, like offender profiling, is known by other names including comparative case analysis and linkage analysis. In contrast to offender profiling case linkage is more widely practised, although little has been reported about it in the popular media. In research terms, it has not received the same degree of attention as offender profiling. While the first study to consider whether crime series could be identified through their behavioural similarity was published in 1976, it is only since 2001 that it has been researched with any fervour.

As we saw above, offender profiling is typically conducted by consulting psychologists, whereas police personnel such as crime analysts usually conduct case linkage. While it is often used in the investigation of serious crimes, such as stranger sex offences and murder, case linkage is also applied to volume crime such as robbery and burglary. The police can use it for several purposes. First, it can increase the efficiency of police investigations, allowing police officers to work together and combine their investigative efforts and resources. Second, it can and has been used as similar fact evidence in Court (which relates to the issue of whether several crimes were perpetrated by the same person).

Case linkage has also been applied to the historical and infamous case of Jack the Ripper in an attempt to determine how many of the Whitechapel murders this mysterious character committed.

This case study illustrates some of the key processes involved in case linkage: the crime analyst must consider the similarities *and* differences between each pair of crimes in order to assess the likelihood of their being linked. The researchers analysing the Whitechapel murders also considered the rarity of the behaviours displayed in the murders. This is an important step in the case

CASE STUDY

Linking the crimes of Jack the Ripper

In the late nineteenth century in London, eleven women were murdered in an area called Whitechapel. At the time this was an area of poverty and disease and the gruesome murders caused great fear among the local people. The murders occurred at night, most outside on the streets of Whitechapel although one occurred inside a house in the area. The man thought responsible for these murders has never been identified but has been given the name Jack the Ripper.

There has been a great deal of speculation about the true identity of the murderer. A quick web search indicates this, resulting in numerous web pages where you can find details about the various suspects. How many of the eleven murders can be attributed to Jack the Ripper has also been debated.

Recently, academics from the University of Washington and Sam Houston State University, in the US, have tried to answer this question by analysing the newly released police files on these murders. Through focusing on the behaviours of the perpetrator(s) the researchers linked six of the eleven murders together based on the similarity of behaviour. The careful planning that had gone into them, the extensive cutting of the victims, the mutilation of the victims' bodies, and the posing of their bodies in sexually degrading manners in preparation for their discovery, were highlighted as the consistent and distinctive features. Such behaviours were not apparent in the other five murders that occurred in the Whitechapel area at that time. On comparing this collection of behaviours to a database of US murders, the specific combination of behaviours displayed in these six murders was found to be very rare and hence the researchers concluded that six of the eleven murders could be attributed to Jack the Ripper with some confidence.

linkage process. While there might be obvious similarities between a pair of crimes if the shared behaviours commonly occur, this does not strongly suggest that the crimes were committed by the same person. Because we may have misconceptions about which behaviours are a rare or common occurrence for a type of crime it is important to work this out statistically by consulting databases of crimes.

As with offender profiling, if case linkage is to be considered a scientific practice it is important that it has a sound theoretical basis. It is to the psychological assumptions of case linkage that we now turn.

assumptions of case linkage

The theoretical grounding of the practice of case linkage comes from personality psychology. To be able to identify a series of offences committed by the same offender based on the behaviour displayed requires the offender to be consistent in his or her offending behaviour. Case linkage, like offender profiling, therefore rests on the Offender Consistency Hypothesis. As noted above, the evidence supporting this assumption is growing.

In addition, case linkage assumes that offenders' offending behaviour will be distinctive from one another's. (If all offenders were consistent in their behaviour but in the same way it would be impossible to distinguish one offender's crimes from another offender's crimes.) To test this second criterion for case linkage, researchers have tried statistically to distinguish pairs of crimes committed by the same offender (linked pairs) from pairs of crimes committed by different offenders (unlinked pairs). Samples of linked offences have been developed by sampling the offences of serial offenders. 'Linked' offences are therefore those that are known to have been committed by the same offender, usually as a result of conviction. (Clearly there is potential for error with this indicator).

Researchers using various statistical techniques have investigated whether linked pairs could be differentiated from unlinked pairs based on measures of behavioural similarity. In all studies conducted thus far this goal has been achieved. The research has also striven to identify whether linked and unlinked offences can be differentiated using similarity in certain behaviours compared to other behaviours. Similarity in behaviours related to controlling the victim/witnesses and the distance travelled to commit crimes have performed better as predictors of linkage than variables relating to how the target was selected, the planning of the offence or the property stolen.

As noted above, one common limitation of offender profiling techniques is that the relationships between offender behaviours and offender characteristics have been developed from samples of known offenders. This is also a limitation of the research for case linkage.

evaluations of the practice of case linkage

Research into case linkage is really only just beginning, which is surprising since it is widely practised and has been for some time. While no studies have examined its effectiveness prospectively, and no consumer satisfaction surveys have been completed, one study looked at the decision-making of investigators conducting case linkage. Four groups of participants were asked to try and identify which of fifteen car crimes belonged to which of five offenders (each offender had committed three car crimes). They were then asked to repeat this task with a different set of fifteen car crimes belonging to five other offenders. All participants were provided with the police crime reports and maps of the relevant crime scenes. One group consisted of experienced car crime investigators, another of experienced investigators of another type of crime, the third group consisted of inexperienced investigators, and a fourth of naïve/lay people. During the linking task participants were asked to articulate the decisions they were making and they were also later questioned on this topic. The naïve group was significantly less accurate at linking than the other three groups who did not differ from each other.

In relation to the information processed, the experienced car-crime investigators focused on a smaller number of variables for linkage than the other groups. On examining which variables were associated with the correct linking of cases and which were associated with incorrect linking, more context-dependent variables resulted in less accuracy (e.g. property taken). In contrast, the use of behaviours that could be considered more inherent to the offender, such as type of vehicle targeted and time of taking, was associated with more accurate linkage.

conclusions

Criminal psychology is an exciting field in which to research and work. Offender profiling in particular has captured the interest of the public and students of criminal psychology alike. In contrast to its portrayal in the popular media, it is a field in its infancy which still requires a lot of development, particularly in relation to establishing a solid theoretical base and evaluating its effectiveness in a methodologically rigorous way. Similarly, while case linkage has also received research attention it is a developing field and one that perhaps does not lend itself as well to exciting dramatization: hence its absence from popular media. Research to test its assumptions is showing promising results. However, practitioners of offender profiling and case linkage should proceed with caution until further research is conducted.

recommended further reading

Ainsworth, P. (2001) *Offender profiling and crime analysis.* London: Willan Publishing.

Alison, L. J. (ed.) (2005) *The forensic psychologist's casebook: Psychological profiling and criminal investigation.* Cullompton, UK: Willan.

Alison, L. J., Bennell, C., Mokros, A. and Ormerod, D. (2002) The personality paradox in offender profiling: A theoretical review of the processes involved in deriving background characteristics from crime scene actions. *Psychology, Public Policy and Law, 8,* 115–35.

Bennell, C. and Jones, N. J. (2005) Between a ROC and a hard place: A method for linking serial burglaries by modus operandi. *Journal of Investigative Psychology and Offender Profiling, 2,* 23–41.

Canter, D. (2000) Offender profiling and criminal differentiation. *Legal and Criminological Psychology, 5,* 23–46.

Canter, D. and Alison, L. J. (eds) (1999) *Profiling in policy and practice.* Aldershot, UK: Ashgate.

Grubin, D., Kelly, P. and Brunsdon, C. (2001) *Linking serious sexual assaults through behaviour.* London: Home Office Research Development and Statistics Directorate.

Hazelwood, R. R. and Warren, J. I. (2003) Linkage analysis: Modus operandi, ritual and signature in serial sexual crime. *Aggression and Violent Behavior, 8,* 587–98.

Jackson, J. L. and Bekerian, D. A. (eds) (1997) *Offender profiling: Theory, research and practice.* Chichester, UK: John Wiley and Sons.

Mischel, W. and Shoda, Y. (1995) A cognitive-affective system theory of personality: Reconceptualizing situations, dispositions, dynamics and invariance in personality structure. *Psychological Review, 102,* 246–68.

Rossmo, D. K. (2001) *Geographical profiling.* London: CRC Press.

policing

This chapter offers an overview of some core issues concerning criminal psychology and policing. It will review the general features of the police role, how this has changed over time and how these changes are reflected in the police image. The chapter also considers how police officers cope with the demands placed on them and how personnel are selected, and discusses some of the Government's aims to create a police service representative of the community it serves. Finally, this chapter will explore citizens' perceptions of the police and other police and security agencies, track some of the key developments in the private security industry over the last decade and discuss some forms of voluntary policing, both within and outside the limits of the law.

It might be thought that the roles and responsibilities of the police are well known and agreed upon, but an independent committee of inquiry into the roles and responsibilities of the police in England and Wales (1996) found that no such consensus actually existed. They proposed the following: 'the purpose of the police service is to uphold the law fairly and firmly; to prevent crime; to pursue and bring to justice those who break the law; to keep the Queen's peace; to protect, help, and reassure the community; and to be seen to do this with integrity, common sense and sound judgement'.

Even this description is not without problems, for it is difficult for any definition to capture the vast array of duties performed by the police. Every day the police service is involved in a large range of activities, ranging from fairly trivial tasks such as giving directions to dealing with serious road accidents, reporting deaths to loved ones and investigating crime.

It could be argued that much of what the police do on a daily basis is in fact unrelated to crime.

Police officers not only perform a vast range of 'social service' duties, but work and interact with a variety of people within the criminal justice system, including offenders, informants, suspects, victims, witnesses, lawyers, solicitors, social workers, senior officers and staff at judicial proceedings when officers attend court to give evidence. This diversity of responsibilities is probably one of the main reasons why the media, especially television dramas, focus so much on policing.

In fact it may be questioned whether there are any clear limits to the responsibilities of the police. They perform many routine yet important duties within society, but to what extent is it reasonable to expect the police to work in extremely demanding conditions? Is there an expectation that police officers are 'superhuman', unable to be harmed in the line of duty, akin to some type of superhero? There are numerous examples of very brave emergency service officers across the world who have carried out their duty with extraordinary professionalism and courage. One has only to consider the brave men and women who entered the Twin Towers in New York on 9/11.

When there is a natural disaster looming, is it realistic to expect officers to stay in the environment in order to 'police'? When news of hurricane Katrina alerted the citizens of New Orleans in the US the whole city was ordered to evacuate, but police officers were expected to stay and wait for the hurricane: to remain at the site, live in terrible conditions and leave their families, in order to keep law and order. Is this a reasonable expectation?

In many countries what constitutes routine police activities has been transformed over the last thirty years, reflecting the changing character of the environment being policed.

38 criminal psychology: a beginner's guide

Recent advances in technology have changed the way many crimes are investigated, and the type of evidence that can be produced to bring an offender to justice. The most notable example of this is DNA profiling. Currently the British national DNA databank matches over 1,000 DNA profiles every week. This helps the police to identify criminals, make arrests earlier and obtain more secure convictions. Not only can it be used in the investigation and as evidence in court for current crimes, but also for old unsolved cases. It has also had a significant effect on what are termed 'miscarriages of justice', whereby innocent people have been convicted for a crime they did not commit (see chapter 8). An example of this is the case known as the 'Cardiff Three'.

The Cardiff Three were convicted in 1988 for the brutal murder of a prostitute in Cardiff. Twenty year-old Lynette White was stabbed more than fifty times in a flat above a betting shop and in 1990 three men were sentenced to life imprisonment for her murder. The convictions were overturned by the Court of Appeal in 1992, after new DNA evidence was uncovered under layers of paint on a skirting board in Miss White's flat. This led to the capture of Jeffrey Gafoor, the real murderer, who was jailed for life in 2003. Serious problems regarding the initial police handling of the case were also voiced.

As crime evolves into new areas, for example into new forms of fraud or Internet crime, so police need to continuously respond to the changing needs and challenges. New methods of policing develop (e.g. via CCTV) and specialist units emerge. Even the image of the police has changed. The 'golden era' of policing of the 1950s was personified by the friendly, local bobby on the beat. This image has remained in the public consciousness despite drastic changes in the style of policing. The old image of the bobby walking down the street, knowing the names of citizens within the community and being very much part of the community has changed considerably, although it is still felt that there is a strong association between a uniformed police presence and public confidence.

Historically a strong association has developed between the police uniform and the maintenance of personal and public standards. These concerns have remained important since Peel-style policing began in England in 1829. In the United States, it was well-expressed in the following address to the NYPD by the General Superintendent, Amos Pilsbury, in 1859, which is displayed at the New York Police History Museum, Manhattan, New York:

> The uniform you wear should be a perpetual 'coat of mail' to guard you against every temptation to which you may be exposed, by reminding you that no act of misconduct, or breach of discipline, can escape public observation and censure. By exemplary conduct and manly deportment, you will command the respect and cordial support of all good citizens. For the faithful performance of the important trusts committed to your care, you will be noticed approvingly, and your services will be appreciated by the community.

In England and Wales, the 'bobby' remains a powerful symbol. Few other police forms can project such a compelling image that is easily recognized beyond their own jurisdiction. An exploration of the history of the British police shows that same key concerns have recurred throughout its existence, such as that of ensuring the recognition and distinctiveness of police officers – called 'visibility' – and maintaining a strong supportive relationship with members of the community – known as 'reassurance'. Other concerns have related to the style of policing, the manner in which the police engage with the public and seek their assistance and cooperation in carrying out the law, known as 'engagement'. The occasional public outcries for a return to a significant visible policing presence on the street put the police service under pressure to continually monitor and modify their evolving style of policing, and to ensure that they remain readily identifiable, distinctive and accessible to the public.

The uniforms of the modern police service include anything from full body armour for public order incidents, to specialist firearms equipment and clothing, to variations to the traditional uniform, with perhaps the addition of a bulletproof vest and Doctor Marten style boots! Increasingly attention is being paid to the ways in which the public make sense of the messages sent out by policing activity. Her Majesty's Inspectors of Police commented in 2001 that 'A police officer in uniform on an unhurried foot patrol suggests that "all is well with the world". However a marked police vehicle with blue light and sirens activated sends out a different message. This is currently visible policing but we would suggest it is far from reassuring.'

stress

It is not surprising that the stress experienced by police officers has become the subject of research, for the policing role requires that they deal with difficult situations and investigations, sometimes in highly dangerous and unpredictable circumstances. This is a worldwide problem. The effect of routine stressors over long periods of time can have many detrimental effects, such as medical problems, absenteeism, high staff turnover, alcohol problems, marital problems and family breakdowns.

There is, however, some disagreement on how 'stress' can be defined or measured. Little is known about the causal route from experiencing stress to becoming ill. Different groups may be more susceptible to stress than others. As noted by Brown and Campbell (1994), it is important to establish two major issues: first, whether police work is inherently stressful; and second, whether police officers are adversely affected by exposure to work related stressors.

It may be that police work is inherently stressful, but that does not necessarily mean that officers will always suffer because of it. The dominant policing ideology emphasizes that officers should be capable and emotionally strong individuals, who are able to deal with situations that 'civilians' would find stressful. If the work itself is inherently stressful then what could be done to reduce or remove its causes and effects?

Is police work more stressful than the work of other professions? Violence and aggression are usually assumed to play a significant contribution to stress in the workplace, but other occupations experience similar stressors, notably other emergency services, for example ambulance crews and accident and emergency (casualty) departments. Direct comparisons are difficult largely because of the wide and increasing diversity of policing duties.

Police may witness death and mutilation, and may have to report to family members about the death of a loved one, or deal with violent offenders, and have to respond immediately to dangerous or potentially life-threatening situations. While such traumatic experiences are infrequent, the high levels of uncertainty may in themselves be stressful.

It has been found that not all officers experience the same type or the same level of stress. Different ranks of officers have different causes of stress. Senior ranking officers experience greater organizational pressures relating to administration and paperwork, such as staff shortages, high staff turnover, a lack of resources, high workload and keeping up to date with new developments and techniques. Lower ranks are more susceptible to stress from active police work, such as attending serious traffic accidents and dealing with violent confrontations.

Police are required to maintain a public and private image. Their own police subculture, also known as 'canteen culture', stems largely from a police force historically drawn from white working class males. This canteen culture has certain pronounced features which serve to protect them and provide a sense of mutual support, but emphasizes a macho image and excludes admitting failures, fears and discussing problems, or admitting to experiencing stress. Over time this culture has been passed down, and despite many changes in the service over the last twenty years, many researchers note that canteen culture still exists and may prevent officers from seeking help.

Minority groups within the police service, such as women, or members of ethnic minority groups, may experience the extra stressors of discrimination from members of the public and/or within the organization.

special situations

Beyond their normal duties police are often called in to special situations that require a coordinated response to a civilian disaster or violent incident, for example the Hillsborough Stadium disaster, the Brixton riots, or the 1980s miners' strike. Below is an excerpt taken from a news report from the BBC, which gives some insight into the policing experience of such an event. Bill King was a Chief Inspector at the time of the miners' strike.

> We usually left our families on a Sunday, getting on a coach with all the other officers, returning the following Friday – there was a lot of couples who separated in police families that year. We were usually living in such places as drill halls, sometimes sleeping on the floor, living out of a kitbag. Breakfast was usually taken at about 1 a.m., so that we could be at the pits before dawn. Days were long and tiring, usually returning to our accommodation in the afternoons, to a hot meal and then bed, only to get up again at about midnight. We were all young and fit, but this routine tired us all out so that at the end of the week we got off the coaches like old men. Duty during the day usually consisted of long periods of waiting, or travelling, or talking to the pickets, interspersed with short periods of violence or pushing and shoving with the pickets. The exception was that week at Hatfield, when there was a great deal more action and violence than normal. I remember it very well: being dog tired; long, long working days; very early starts in the morning; the bitterness and understandable abuse from the crowds. I remember the sheer torrent of stones raining down – the sky just fell on us with stones, sticks, bits of railings, bricks, ball bearings. At one point I looked up and the sky was black with missiles. I felt the weight of command and concern for my officers and personal fear at the level of violence from the crowd, mixed with the excitement of the situation. I lost a stone in weight that week and I found holes in the soles of both my shoes by the end of it.

Police are more likely than most other professions to be confronted with shocking or unexpected events. These one-off traumatic events may have a profound and devastating effect. It is normal to experience some stress and to be upset by devastating incidents, but if these symptoms (such as experiencing flashbacks of the incident, sleep problems, feelings of detachment and disruption to normal life) persist over a long period of time, then an officer may be suffering from post-traumatic stress disorder (PTSD).

Recent disasters such as bombings and train crashes, have drawn attention and raised awareness of the fact that the police and other emergency services experience such devastating incidents. Preparation for the management of such disasters, physically, operationally and psychologically, is difficult. It is increasingly acknowledged that participation in such traumatic incidents requires a great deal of support from within the police organization.

Coping with stress can be attempted at an individual or organizational level. It is well known that stress impairs social, physical and psychological functioning and can result in errors, accidents and poor judgement. It may be experienced as feeling of tension, anxiety, irritability, poor concentration or sleeplessness, and can affect relationships with family, friends and colleagues. It depresses the immune system making people more susceptible to physical illnesses, such as heart disease, stomach ulcers, migraines and high blood pressure, and is associated with alcohol or drug dependency, an increased rate of marital breakdown and even suicide.

Research suggests that many police officers hide their symptoms, often with the cumulative effect of declining health and impaired job performance. Informal methods of coping, such as the black humour of the canteen culture, provide only short-term alleviation for many. As policing becomes increasingly stressful, there is greater interest in the topic of stress management and counselling for traumatic incidents. Training to prepare officers and maintain officers' ability to manage stressful encounters is vital. Providing psychological support for officers, including specially designed programmes, is crucial.

personnel selection (including specialist units)

Given the role the police play in society and the potentially stressful environment in which they will be placed, a thorough selection process for new recruits is essential to the maintenance and improvement of the service. Undesirable characteristics such as racist and sexist attitudes must be identified early in the selection process, so that applicants exhibiting such characteristics are not invited to join the police service.

The screening in and screening out of applicants is done via a variety of methods such as psychometric tests, interviews, role-play, attendance to assessment centres, fitness tests and medical tests. There is some dispute as to whether performances on these tests can predict actual future performance or success as a police officer, which is not surprising considering how difficult it would be to measure police success, or even what characteristics would describe a good police officer in the first place. This is particularly significant given the wide range of roles police officers perform.

'Faking good' refers to successful candidates on some tests simply faking it in order to succeed. It is for reasons such as these that some people suggest that psychometric tests are not particularly useful in screening candidates in or out. Support for such testing has also declined over the years because it is difficult to agree on exactly what qualities would make a good police officer and, where there is any agreement, these traits are often very difficult to measure.

Selection deals not only with new recruits, but also experienced officers wanting to be promoted or move into more specialist areas, such as firearms, bomb disposal, public order or CID. Again the debate arises as to what the essential personal attributes required for success in these different roles might be and how they should be measured.

So what are suitable characteristics for police officers? Psychological research suggests traits such as good interpersonal skills, common sense, assertiveness, a good sense of humour, honesty, problem-solving and sensitivity – but these traits are difficult to quantify and predict. Many people suggest that there is a certain 'type' of person or personality that become police officers because particular types of people are attracted to this occupation. The training can also shape the recruits' behaviour.

a police personality?

Researching the possible existence of the 'police personality' is important both in terms of who would be best suited to particular duties and who can cope with particular stressors. There is no conclusive evidence as to the origins of the police personality, but research evidence does suggest that such a 'personality' does exist and that the police do differ from other occupational groups. Traits such as authoritarianism, dogmatism, conservatism and cynicism appear to be present in policing samples, but whether applicants join the service with such a personality or whether it is the police training that shapes officers' behaviour is difficult to determine. The evidence available suggests that it stems more from police training rather than the attitude of people when entering the police service. Several studies have demonstrated that authoritarianism, for example, develops as officers gained experience on the beat.

The reasons why people choose to join the police service and their initial motivations is an area that is under-researched. The reasons why some officers remain and thrive in the service for a full career while others drop out are not well understood at this time.

a police service representing the community it serves

The demographic composition of the police service in many countries has changed considerably over the last thirty years, reflecting the change in composition of the population and wider changes in society. The police service, like many other organizations, is now actively involved with issues of equality and diversity. This requires that career opportunities and promotion are open to everyone within society regardless of age, gender, sexual orientation, race, religious beliefs or disability. In this way the skills, knowledge and experience of the organization can be vastly improved and a better service offered to all.

Historically, women have not always been permitted to become involved in policing. In Britain women were first involved with policing activities during the First World War, largely in the role of volunteer work, and mainly involved in moral guidance and crime prevention patrols near munitions factories. By the Second World War women were involved in a wider range of duties, revolving around clerical and supportive duties and general housekeeping activities. After the Second World War women were employed to carry out what could be classed as 'caring' duties requiring sensitivity and good interpersonal skills, such as dealing with lost children and domestic violence. In 1975 the Sex Discrimination Act passed into law and women were entitled to full employment rights. By 2003, there were 25,390 female officers working in England and Wales. Women are now employed in every aspect of policing, including firearms, public order and CID, and the country now has several female chief constables (i.e. chiefs of police).

Police services in several countries have also been attempting to actively recruit citizens from ethnic minority groups: the aim being to provide a police service that is representative of the community it serves. However, targets may be particularly difficult to reach not only in terms of attracting new recruits to the force, but in maintaining them, as research shows that large numbers of the ethnic minority recruits leave within two years of joining. This may be in part due to perceptions of 'institutional racism', a label given to the police following racist disruptions in Britain. However, Lord Scarman's Report of 1981 (following the Brixton Riots) and the Macpherson Report (following the murder of Stephen Lawrence, 1993) both acknowledge not only the problems of racism and racially motivated crime throughout Britain, but also the concept of institutional racism within the police service itself.

In his report Lord Scarman responded to the suggestion that 'Britain is an institutionally racist society':

> If, by [institutionally racist] it is meant that it [Britain] is a society which knowingly, as a matter of policy, discriminates against black people, I reject the allegation. If, however, the suggestion being made is that practices may be adopted by public bodies as

well as private individuals which are unwittingly discriminatory against black people, then this is an allegation which deserves serious consideration, and, where proved, swift remedy.

Some recent developments show evidence of commitment to provide equality and diversity to all prospective applicants including gay and lesbian citizens. In England and Wales the Gay Police Association was set up in 1990. Recently it has been working towards introducing a sexual orientation scheme, in order to monitor the sexual orientation of all its staff. Clearly not all staff may wish to divulge such personal information, but it does offer staff members the choice to do so if they wish. The Gay Police Association aims to support gay staff and to educate the police service and central government on issues connected with sexual orientation and policing. This includes policy development, the investigation of homophobic hate crime, victim care, and community liaison. It is estimated that there are over 5.8 million members of the public throughout England and Wales who are lesbian or gay. Having officers of diverse sexual orientation may improve the service provided to the community, especially for those who may feel marginalized or victimized because of their sexuality.

public perceptions of the police

Police forces in many countries enjoy a positive relationship with the public. Despite periods of unrest, allegations of racism, sexism and awkward interactions with youths, citizens in such countries generally have trust and respect for the police. Both police and citizens support the concept that effective policing requires public support, therefore to provide a professional police service the police must work with the community. Many writers believe that it is the notion of 'policing by consent' that is the hallmark of British policing. The British police are proud to remain routinely unarmed, retain the principal of minimum force and carry a minimal amount of equipment for their own protection. Throughout its history the British police has worked on the principle of being unarmed, uniformed citizens.

Perhaps the ever-increasing demands for more police on the street is a reflection of the positive relationship the public have with the police. In Britain there are often calls for more uniformed police on the street, which research suggests offers citizens reassurance, lowers fear of crime and maintains law and order.

However, years of intelligence-led policing, large amounts of paperwork, the introduction of cars and the increasing amount of specialist functions (such as fraud, Internet crime etc.) have taken the police off the street and out of the sight of the public. This has resulted in a greater demand for a uniformed presence on the streets which has been recognized by recent Government policy documents.

Together with the perception that the police are being removed from public view, other changes have occurred in society that have resulted in a greater need for security. Over the last fifty years or so there has been a massive increase in the amount of land, property and possessions that citizens own (and many of these possessions such as DVD players, laptops, mobile phones and televisions are also very easily transportable), making it easier for thieves to steal, transport and then sell on. All sorts of security products are available to help citizens to protect their homes and possessions (e.g. burglar alarms, bolts and locks), and this industry has become big business. Presumably the more fearful people are the more security they will need.

Security has also been developed in terms of manned guards. In recent years commercialism has grown, and so has the need for shop owners to protect the premises against shoplifters and trouble makers. This has resulted in uniformed private security guards interacting with the public on a day to day basis. In fact in many countries the private security industry has developed its services at a staggering rate and conducts a diverse range of activities. There has been some concern about the increasing role these security agencies play in relation to the public, especially as until recently there was no legislation in England and Wales in place to regulate or control the private security industry. This has resulted in some very interesting research uncovering the darker side of the industry, such as bouncers dealing drugs, the 'night-time economy', and many cases of criminals running security companies in order to exploit their perceived authority. To prevent further abuse and risk to the public, the Private Security Industry Act was established in 2001. The industry is now regulated and only accredited officers are allowed to perform security duties.

Other changes that made a significant difference to citizens' lifestyles and policing activity is the merging of public and private space. Over the last twenty years there has been a vast increase in public access to privately owned premises such as shopping malls and leisure centres. As more activities take place on private property, more private security is required to protect it. The roles of the police and private security organizations increasingly overlap, and the boundaries of 'private' and 'public' have become less clear.

Despite an increase over the last twenty years in the types and number of uniformed officers the public are now likely to see on the streets, citizens still want more police on the street. In order to fulfil this need in England and Wales the government has introduced a number of schemes to provide this uniformed presence, but these are not necessarily police as we have known them in the past. Many schemes have been set up over the last decade, such as Neighbourhood Warden Schemes, and more recently Police Community Support Officers (PCSOs). PCSOs do not have the same powers as police or the same extensive training, but they do wear a uniform that is remarkably similar to that of a police officer and do work with the police. So far the government have been so pleased with the work of PCSOs that it plans to increase the numbers from 6,214 currently to at least 25,000 by 2008.

Throughout England and Wales in 2003 there were 141,230 police officers and 12,077 special constables (part-time, volunteer officers). In comparison, according to the Security Industry Authority in 2003, there were approximately half a million security officers working in the private security industry, with an annual revenue of 3–4 billion pounds. Clearly, policing and security are in great demand.

This chapter has dealt mainly with issues regarding public police and private security. However, there is a vast array of policing activities conducted by many other agencies that fall outside these two categories and it is increasingly difficult to group or categorize these agencies. They all have different roles and responsibilities and work within different boundaries of the law. For example, private investigators are not bound by the same stringent rules as police officers, and they have many methods of investigation open to them. Many of the large investigation firms have the most advanced technology available, can access sophisticated databases, and use perhaps what could be described as 'less ethical' methods of investigation (such as delving through someone's rubbish bins and tapping phone lines) in order to gather information for their client.

Voluntary policing is also an area of great interest, but has received little attention from academics. British criminologist Professor Les Johnston is one of the few who have conducted research in this area. He divides voluntary policing into two categories, which he terms 'responsible citizenship' and 'autonomous citizenship'. Responsible citizenship includes citizens working within the guidelines of the law, such as those volunteering as special constables or becoming involved in local neighbourhood watch. Within this category Johnston (1996) also discusses 'spontaneous citizen involvement', whereby a citizen may witness a crime taking place and intervene or report it. However, clearly there is scope here for citizens to become too involved and become a 'have-a-go-hero' (Johnston 1996). The mass media may also play a role in investigation under the umbrella of 'responsible citizenship' (Johnston 1996). The media can gather information from the public to help the police solve crime. The media can also pursue their own investigations, and reporters often go under cover, gathering information and footage to publicize.

The second category suggested by Johnston is 'autonomous citizenship'. This involves citizens setting up their own patrols. There are some well-known examples of this, for example the Guardian Angels in New York. Research suggests that during the 1980s New Yorkers felt safer due to the Guardian Angels' presence, more so than when the police (NYPD) patrolled. Another aspect to autonomous citizenship is 'vigilantism', which involves citizens taking the law into their own hands. This will be discussed in chapter 8 on punishment.

conclusion

It is clear that the police deal with a diverse range of duties, and are 'an all purpose social service' (Morgan and Newburn 1998, p. 75). These duties have developed over the years, new specialist units have emerged, and new tools of investigation and technology help the police solve crime (e.g. CCTV and DNA). Society and policing have changed, and the image of policing image reflects this.

There appears to be no limit to the public expectation of police responsibilities, and it is not surprising that police stress has been researched by psychologists. Research suggests that police do experience stress, and the most common coping strategy reported appears to be talking to colleagues.

It has been suggested that only certain types of people are attracted to working in the police service, and this raises the question whether there is a 'police personality'. Research supports this view, as there do appear to be common traits amongst police officers, such as authoritarianism. Research is still examining whether this is as a result of police training or because some personality types are simply drawn to policing.

This chapter also considered the Government's aims to provide a police service representative of the community it serves drawing on examples of minority groups including women, ethnic minorities and sexual orientation. While there is a clear message that these citizens would be greatly encouraged, it is difficult to envisage how the Government could really meet its targets, firstly in terms of attracting enough recruits, and secondly in retaining them.

Finally, the chapter considered developments in public policing arrangements (e.g. the introduction of PCSOs), the huge growth of the private security industry in Britain and various forms of voluntary policing. Clearly the public police do not have a monopoly on policing and security, and the future of policing will involve many different agencies, transforming the way citizens are policed, crime is investigated and evidence is provided to bring offenders to justice.

recommended further reading

Brown, J. M. and Campbell, E. A. (1994) *Stress and policing.* Chichester: Wiley.

Button, M. (2002) *Private policing.* Cullompton, UK: Willan.

Johnston, L. (1996) What is vigilantism? *British Journal of Criminology, 36,* 220–36.

Kapardis, A. (2001) *Psychology and the law: A critical introduction.* Cambridge: Cambridge University Press.

Morgan, R. and Newburn, T. (1998) *The future of policing.* Oxford: Oxford University Press.

online resources

http://www.homeoffice.gov.uk
The Home office web site, which has a large section on policing.

http://www.police.uk
The UK police service web site.

interviewing suspects and witnesses

confessions

Societies expect that their police service will protect them from wrongdoers, especially dangerous criminals, and police forces strive hard to achieve this. One of the major ways in which they seek to do this is by apprehending the criminals and getting them to confess to their crimes. Unfortunately, this commendable striving to get the guilty to confess also has a number of negative effects.

Two important drawbacks of too strong a focus on confessions are that (i) innocent people do confess to crimes they have not committed (i.e. false confessions) and (ii) guilty people might confess but, if the police do not also strive to gather other evidence against them (e.g. in their interviews), when some of these later retract their confession there is little else that courts can use against them.

We will soon look at the explanations criminal psychologists have developed to help explain the puzzle of why innocent people confess. But how do we know that innocent people confess? One way involves modern uses of DNA that check whether 'biological' traces left by the criminal (e.g. in hair, semen, and so on) match the confessor. Ongoing work in the USA called the 'Innocence Project' examines cases of people imprisoned for crimes that they claim they did not commit. At the time of the crime some years ago a biological trace was left by the perpetrator but this DNA trace was too small to be analysed by the time of the trial at which a person was found guilty (i.e. on other evidence). However, recent advances in DNA testing now allow much smaller samples to be tested than was the case even a few years ago. If the police and/or the authorities (to their credit) have safely preserved the small sample it might now be amenable to testing. The Innocence Project has now done just this and in well over one hundred cases the DNA of the person in prison has been found not to match the crime sample. When the case files of these imprisoned people have been examined it has been found (i) that the most frequent type of evidence against them was eyewitness testimony (see chapter 6) and (ii) that in around twenty per cent of cases the person now shown to be innocent actually confessed to the police.

Another way of demonstrating that false confessions do occur is by examining individual cases in which people have confessed and have been found guilty on this basis by a court of law only for it to be demonstrated years later that they were not the guilty party. Gudjonsson's (2003) book provides details of several such cases.

So what are the explanations that criminal psychologists have offered to explain false confessions? One rather obvious reason is that some (probably a minority) are voluntary – innocent people confess, for example, to gain notoriety or to cover up for a friend. Another explanation, which involves more psychology, is that under pressure people will sometimes agree to things simply to relieve the pressure (e.g. torture, solitary confinement). Such confessions are called 'coerced-compliant', partly because the false confessors still know they did not do it. Most worrying are 'coerced-internalized' false confessions in which the confessors themselves actually come to believe that they must have done it. For these, the psychological explanation is more complex and can involve special vulnerability on the part of the confessor (e.g. due to low intelligence, high anxiety, low maturity and/or a number of psychological/mental disorders). However, such vulnerabilities are not enough to explain this phenomenon. Poor, or should we say old-fashioned, police interview methods have been shown, time and again, to have resulted in coerced false confessions.

Research has demonstrated that unless trained to the contrary most police officers who are about to interview suspects already believe that it is highly likely that the suspect is the person who committed the crime. This is so even when the available information indicating this to be so is poor or weak. Given this prior belief in guilt, it is not surprising that such officers see their main role as the securing of a confession. Unfortunately, in most countries in the world, the officers do not actively seek to gather information from the suspects within the interviews that can reliably be used to guide the decision as to whether the confession is a true one or a false one.

In some countries (e.g. the USA) many police forces currently train their officers to interview suspects in two main stages. The first stage (often called 'the interview') is designed to allow suspects to say whether they committed the crime or not. Some do admit to it. For those who do not, a decision is made during stage one as to whether they are lying when saying that they did not do it. Those deemed to be lying then enter stage two (often called 'the interrogation') which is designed to persuade/pressurize them to admit it. Police officers using this two-stage approach base much of their stage one decision as to whether the denying suspect is lying or not on an examination of the suspect's behaviour. Most unfortunately, the cues they are trained to look for, while relating commonsense beliefs about lying (see the next chapter for more on this), are not valid. Thus, they misclassify innocent deniers as liars and then put pressure on them to confess. This pressure is designed to gain confessions (for more on this see Kassin, 2005) and therefore, not surprisingly, many people confess, especially those who are vulnerable to pressure. However, those not so affected by psychological pressure (e.g. psychopaths, terrorists, spies, career criminals) may not confess. Some of these may not do so even in the face of ethically and morally questionable procedures involving torture and threats to their families.

It is difficult to determine how often ethically and morally questionable procedures are used on those suspected of wrongdoing. Some suspects later make claims about how they were interviewed/interrogated, but the 'authorities' may deny such claims. However, if the interviews are tape-recorded then it may be possible to obtain a better picture of what actually happened. This is one of the reasons why in England and Wales the Police and Criminal Evidence Act 1984 mandated that all police interviews with suspects be audiotape recorded.

Another reason for this pioneering legislation was to assist the police to determine, via the tape recordings, which aspects of suspect interviewing they were already good at and where there might be room for improvement.

Before we examine studies of tape-recorded interviews with suspects, let us look at one of the few published studies in which a researcher was allowed to sit in on police interviews with suspects. Other similar studies may have been conducted in various countries but have not usually been published. In this 1980 study (which was conducted for the Royal Commission On Criminal Procedure) Barrie Irving was present at several dozen interviews in England. He noted that the interviewers used a number of persuasive/manipulative tactics, including:

- pretending to be in possession of more evidence than they actually had
- minimizing the seriousness of the offence
- manipulating the interviewee's self-esteem
- pointing out the futility of denial.

In its 1981 report the Royal Commission expressed concern about these tactics. Not only is lying to the suspect about the evidence ethically questionable (given that the suspect may be innocent), it may also reveal to guilty suspects (who know what happened) that the police are mistaken/lying about the evidence: thus the guilty may be less likely to confess. Furthermore, if the police lie in this context, the general public will learn of this and it may well lessen the positive regard societies need to have of their police service. These are some of the reasons why British courts dissuade police officers from lying to suspects. However, in the USA it seems that the Supreme Court has sanctioned such lying.

This tactic of minimizing the seriousness of the offence can take several forms. One example we heard about (from outside the UK) involved the interview of an uncle accused of the rape of his six-year-old niece. The police interviewer said to him: 'I've had little girls sitting on my lap. They wriggle and before you realise it you've got an involuntary erection. Is that what happened to you and then did it just slip into her?'

Manipulation of the interviewee's self-esteem to lower it so that they become more psychologically vulnerable not only raises ethical concerns but may also result in more false confessions.

Pointing out the futility of denial is designed to stop guilty suspects continuing to deny their involvement, but again this is likely to increase the false confession rate. However, here we should note the point made earlier in this section that in some countries police forces believe that they can tell which suspects are liars/guilty, so they say they use these tactics only on guilty people (who, of course, won't produce false confessions). Discussing the detection of deception, chapter 5 demonstrates that such police beliefs are error-prone.

In light of the 1981 Royal Commission report and UK national media focus on the possibility of false confessions (which, of course, mean that the guilty remain free), the government in England and Wales brought in the 1984 Act which not only mandated the tape recording of interviews with suspects but also aimed to stop the use of inappropriate – coercive, oppressive – tactics, emphasizing that confessions should be voluntary.

A few years after the introduction of the new legislation the government funded a number of studies of tape-recorded interviews with suspects. These (and other published studies conducted by senior police officers as part of their research doctorates – a crucial development) revealed a surprising lack of police skills if the suspect denied the offence. Most suspects who confessed did so near the beginning of their interview (that is, before the interviewers' skills were revealed) and the strength of the (true) evidence against them played a role in this. A major tactic seemed to be to reveal at the beginning of the interview all of the evidence against the suspect and to then tell them to confess. This might work if the evidence is very strong – guilty suspects can tell this and also know that courts might give them a lesser sentence if they confess. However, if the evidence is not strong, the guilty may well realize this and not confess. When the evidence was weak and the suspects did not confess, the research found that the police interviewers did not seem to know what to do. The 1984 Act had resulted in inappropriate psychological tactics rarely being employed but had not provided the police with alternative procedures.

To their credit, the police service took note of the research findings and in 1992 produced a national training interviewing initiative which took the trouble to be informed by criminal psychology. This pioneering initiative (nothing like it appears to have happened in other countries) emphasized that in interviews with suspects the role of the police is (i) to gather accurate information, (ii) to keep an open mind, (iii) to act fairly, especially with vulnerable suspects, (iv) to compare information gained in the interview with other information, (v) to question the suspect appropriately, even if they exercise the right to silence and (vi) to not necessarily accept the first answer given by the suspect. The publication of these principles attempted to change the confession-driven model of suspect interviewing to one involving a search for information.

Accompanying these principles was a training package and two booklets given to all 127,000 police officers in Wales and England. The training and the booklets were extensively based on ethical psychological notions. Some years after their introduction a number of research studies were conducted to assess the new situation. For example, we conducted in-depth interviews with highly experienced detectives about what they considered to be the important skills when interviewing suspects. From what they said and from the relevant research (some of which has been described above) we drew up a questionnaire that a large sample of police interviewers filled in. The results indicated that the police service now considered the following skills to be the most important when interviewing suspects – listening, preparation, questioning, flexibility, open-mindedness and compassion/empathy. Thus the new national initiative seemed to have been successful.

Of course, what people say may differ from what they actually do. We therefore analysed tape-recorded interviews with suspects. Some of these we evaluated as 'good' and some 'not so good'. The skills which were actually more evident in the good interviews included responding to what the interviewee says, use of open questions, flexibility, open-mindedness, compassion/empathy, keeping the interviewee to relevant topics, preparing the interview, appropriate use of pauses/silences, apparent use of (appropriate) tactics, appropriate use of closed questions and communication skills. Thus what the interviewers from several forces said was important was borne out by interviews conducted in those forces (prior to this research project ever starting). However, even in the good interviews, some of these skills were not present that often (e.g. appropriate use of pauses/silences, flexibility and compassion/empathy). On the other hand, even in the not so good interviews some skills were frequently present (e.g. absence of undue pressure, of inappropriate interruptions, of long/complex questions and not releasing all of the information at the beginning).

A few years later we conducted another analysis of real-life tape-recorded interviews with suspects. This found (contrary to the research on interviews conducted before the 1992 training initiative) that most of the confessions did not occur near to the beginning of the interviews. It also found that the problematic tactics of minimization, situational futility (i.e. telling the suspect that they committed this crime and that it will come out one day, and pointing out the negative consequences of denial) and intimidation never occurred. The tactics that occurred often included 'challenges account' and 'emphasizing contradictions', which had been emphasized in the (new) training initiative. But what about the tactic 'showing concern'? Though this only occurred in a minority of interviews, it may be very important. Certainly, when we asked experienced interviewers what factors are important (see above), they frequently mentioned empathy/compassion. The importance of this skill probably relates to the fundamental question of 'Why should guilty suspects confess to the police?'.

If psychologically (and physically) coercive/oppressive techniques are not to be used in interviews with suspects to motivate them to confess, what will? We were a little puzzled that showing concern seemed to be related to suspects moving from denial to confession. Then we found a study conducted just a few years ago in Sweden that noted that men now in prison for serious crimes such as murder indicated on an extensive question-naire that a humanitarian (rather than a dominating) police interviewing style was related to their decisions to confess in the interviews.

Thus, with regard to the crucial topic of police interviewing of suspects, criminal psychology has been associated (at least in England and Wales) with a turn away from what has been called unethical to ethical policing. A number of countries (e.g. Norway) are now taking note of this.

interviewing witnesses

Some countries have also taken steps designed to improve the interviewing of witnesses, especially (i) those who may have been victims of serious crimes such as sexual abuse and (ii) those who need most help to remember accurately (e.g. children and vulner-able adults). These steps, like the police interviewing of suspects described above, have often accompanied governmental decisions to tape record interviews with alleged victims or bystanders who witnessed what took place.

England and Wales have pioneered the routine video taping of investigative interviews with children. The Criminal Justice Act 1991 allowed a video recorded interview (usually by the police and/or social services) to be used as part of a child's evidence, pro-vided that the judge deemed the interviewing to have been con-ducted appropriately. (The judge could order that some or all of the recording not be shown to the jury.) To provide guidance to interviewers the Government commissioned a Professor of Psychology (Ray Bull) and a Professor of Law (Di Birch) to write the first working draft of the 1992 *Memorandum of Good Practice*

On Video Recorded Interviews With Child Witnesses For Criminal Proceedings (MOGP). This extensive guidance document summarized what was known at the time, largely from psychological research, about how best to interview children, in a user-friendly format. Research from several countries (e.g. Germany, Canada, Australia, the USA) seemed to be in agreement that such interviews should involve a series of sequential phases that could be described as:

- establish rapport,
- obtain free recall,
- ask appropriate questions,
- achieve closure.

This phased approach made it clear that in order to assist children to tell the interviewers as much as possible about what may have happened, the interviewers must first of all devote time to establishing a positive relationship between themselves and the child, but in a way that could not be criticized as serving to bias or unduly influence what the child might say. A wealth of psychological research has demonstrated that to assist people to recall often complex and distressing events, they must be in as positive a frame of mind as possible and have positive regard for the interviewer. (This applies strongly to many aspects of criminal psychology.)

Another body of psychological research has demonstrated that when people are remembering events, what they say in their own words (in psychology this is called 'free recall') is more accurate than what they say in response to questions. Thus, good interviewing first allows witnesses to provide free recall before asking them questions. On the face of it, this might seem easy to do but, in fact, research has repeatedly shown that untrained interviewers interrupt witnesses' free recall with questions. It is actually quite difficult to hold one's questions until the witness has finished his or her free recall. It is important to do so not only because interrupting conveys to the witness that the interviewer wants short accounts, but also because questions run the risk of biasing the replies.

Some question types are more biasing (or suggestive) than others. Leading questions suggest the desired answer. For example, 'You are enjoying reading this book, aren't you?'. Research has shown that children and vulnerable adults are very inclined to reply 'Yes' to leading questions. The problem, therefore, with such questions is that one does not know whether the answer is a true representation of what is in the interviewee's mind or is merely compliance to the question (especially if it is asked by an adult in authority). Thus, the MOGP pointed out that some types of questions were preferable to leading questions. It advised that in the questioning phase 'open' questions should be asked first, then 'specific' questions, then 'closed' questions and preferably no leading questions.

Open questions invite the interviewee to provide information additional to that given in their free recall. For example, 'A few minutes ago you said that your uncle hurt you. How did he do that?'. Specific questions focus on detail. For example, 'You said your uncle pushed something into your mouth. What did he use?'. Closed questions contain a list of alternatives but, of course, they run the risk of not including the correct alternative or of suggesting an alternative (that makes more 'sense' than the other alternatives). Closed questions that contain few (e.g. two) alternatives are especially risky, since research has shown that children and vulnerable adults may choose one of the alternatives even though doing so provides an incorrect account of what happened. One reason why young children do this is because they believe that adults (especially authority figures) already know what happened and that their role (i.e. the children's) is merely to confirm that the adult is correct. This is one of the reasons why the MOGP (and similar guidance documents) emphasizes that the witnesses must be told that the interviewer will be happy if the witness says 'I don't understand' or 'I don't know' (contrary to what school teachers may say).

Leading questions, because they suggest the answer (e.g. 'Your uncle touched your bottom, didn't he?' – when the child has given no indication of this) should rarely, if ever, be used when interviewing witnesses (or suspects). If one is used, it should be followed up not by the use of further leading questions (as often happens in everyday conversations) but by the use of open questions.

Finally, the closing phase has two major parts. The first involves the interviewers checking that they have correctly understood the important parts, if any, of what the interviewees have communicated. The second involves ensuring that the interviewee leaves in as positive a frame of mind as possible (by, for example, returning to some of the neutral topics covered in the rapport phase).

In 2002 the Government in England and Wales published an update of its 1992 (MOGP) guidance document. This extensive update is entitled *Achieving Best Evidence in Criminal Proceedings: Guidance for Vulnerable and Intimidated Witnesses, Including Children (ABE)* and it was written by a team (including criminal psychologists) led by Professor Graham Davies at the University of Leicester School of Psychology. More recently, the Scottish Executive (2004) published similar guidance regarding child witnesses. Such guidance documents play a number of important roles. For example, in June 2005 the Court Of Appeal in London quashed a man's conviction to 18 months imprisonment for indecent assault of an eight-year-old child. The Court decided this largely because the judge in the original trial had not properly directed the jury regarding the defendant's claim that the interviewing by the police of the child was not in accordance with the official guidance document (i.e. *ABE*).

Psychological research has repeatedly demonstrated just how easy it is for inappropriate questions to bias what witnesses say. Over thirty years ago one such experiment found that when asked about the height of a man they had seen, those asked 'How tall was the man?' produced, on average, responses that were twenty-eight centimetres greater than those asked 'How short was the man?'. Other studies have shown that when asked about items that were not in the original event, more people replied 'yes' to questions worded 'Did you see the ...?' than to 'Did you see a ...?'.

The effects of inappropriate questions have been found to be even more pronounced if they are asked by authority figures. For example, our research found that when children were interviewed about an event, they remembered less and more frequently went along with misleading questions if the interviewer looked and behaved authoritatively.

An extensive, international programme of psychological research has, in the last twenty years, developed ways of helping interviewees remember as much as possible about events. One major way is to use what is known as the 'cognitive interview' (which is often referred to as the CI). This procedure involves a number of techniques based on major research findings and theories in cognitive psychology (e.g. concerning how memory works) and in social psychology (e.g. what constitutes good communication skills). For example, the mental reinstatement of context which assists the interviewee to re-instate in their mind key aspects of the original event. These contextual aspects then 'trigger off' (that is, then allow to be recalled) other aspects of the event that otherwise would have been very difficult to retrieve from memory. Another major aspect of the CI is to transfer control of the memory retrieval to the interviewee (e.g. the witness) which involves the interviewer realizing that they should behave in a way that allows (indeed, motivates) the interviewee to think hard, to do most of the talking, and not to be unduly influenced by any biases or expectations that the interviewer may have about what happened. The CI procedure has been found in many studies to help people remember more. In 2005 the author of this chapter was surprised to receive the rare honour for a civilian of a Commendation Certificate from the London Metropolitan Police Service for the guidance provided in the interviewing of a woman who had been raped but who, initially, could recall little of the horrendous event. Among the guidance given to the interviewer (prior to and during the four-hour interview) were aspects of the CI approach.

questioning in court

An important place where the questioning of (alleged) witnesses, victims and suspects also takes place is in criminal courts.

However, relatively few studies have been conducted on this particular topic, probably because of the difficulties of doing so. In the late 1980s we conducted one of the first published studies of questioning of child witnesses in criminal courts in which eighty-nine children were observed giving evidence in forty trials in Glasgow, Scotland. Among the wealth of information gathered was that concerning the appropriateness of the vocabulary used by the lawyers when questioning children of various ages. Those lawyers whose 'side' had called the child witnesses (usually the prosecution) rarely used vocabulary that the children appeared not to understand (this occurred in only twelve per cent of their 'examinations-in-chief'). However, the 'opposing' lawyers did this much more often (in forty per cent of their cross-examinations). The inappropriate vocabulary was by no means directed at only the youngest children. Indeed, for these the lawyers appeared to be conscious of the need to keep their vocabulary simple. (The lawyers also largely used age-appropriate grammar, ninety per cent and eighty-three per cent, respectively.)

However, in other countries the situation may be less appropriate for child witnesses. For example, in New Zealand, the transcripts of twenty child sexual abuse trials in which children aged five to twelve gave evidence (for the prosecution) revealed that the cross-examinations (by the defence lawyers) contained more leading (i.e. suggestive) questions (thirty-five per cent) than did prosecutors' examinations-in-chief (fifteen per cent). Furthermore, (i) children's misunderstanding of questions were evident in sixty-five per cent of the cross-examinations, (ii) there was a relationship between the number of child witness misunderstandings and the defence lawyers' use of complex questions, and (iii) when children appeared to contradict what they had earlier said in the trials this was very often associated with an age-inappropriate question being asked (which caused the contradiction).

The lawyer Emily Henderson claimed that many of the cross-examination tactics used by lawyers to question children are suggestive and are a 'how not to' guide to interviewing (that is, are the opposite of what is contained in guidance documents on how to interview children). She interviewed lawyers in New Zealand and in England who showed good awareness of the dangers of asking suggestive questions, but who still sometimes chose to use them.

A few studies have been published concerning the questioning in court of adult (alleged) victims/witnesses. One looked at the transcripts of rape trials and found that the cross-examinations involved many more 'yes'/'no' questions (which can be suggestive and do constrain the nature of the reply) than the examinations-in-chief (eighty-two per cent vs. forty-seven per cent) but fewer 'open' questions (which allow the witness to give an account not suggested by the question – six per cent versus twenty-three per cent). Another study found similar data for 'ordinary' (alleged) adult rape victims but it also looked at transcripts of trials in which the alleged victims were adults with learning disability (who can have particular difficulty in understanding questions and in resisting suggestive questions). In these latter trials, not only were there many more 'yes'/'no' questions in the cross-examinations, there also were more leading questions than in evidence-in-chief (twenty-five per cent vs. three per cent). In fact, both the defence and prosecution lawyers questioned the witnesses with learning disability in ways similar to ordinary adult rape victims, thus demonstrating no special skills for these particularly vulnerable witnesses. Perhaps this is not surprising because it is only recently that some countries have taken the trouble (i) to encourage particularly vulnerable adults to disclose that they may have been abused, (ii) to train investigative interviewers to interview such people and (iii) to bring in legislation that provides procedures (sometimes referred to as 'special measures') to assist such people to present their evidence to the court (e.g. by the use of video-recorded evidence, live television links from a room to the court room, the use of screens between the witness and the accused).

conclusions

This chapter has examined work by criminal psychologists (and others) that provides guidance on how suspects, witnesses and victims should be interviewed. However, such guidance is only being supported by Governments and other relevant organizations in some countries. Others, sadly, seem ignorant at present of what can now be achieved.

recommended further reading

Carson, D. and Bull, R. (2003) *Handbook of psychology in legal contexts*, 2nd edn. Chichester: Wiley.

Gudjonsson, G. (2003) *The psychology of interrogations and confessions*. Chichester: Wiley.

Home Office (2002) *Achieving best evidence in criminal proceedings: Guidance for vulnerable and intimidated witnesses, including children*. Available at http:/www.cps.gov.uk/publications/prosecution/bestevidencevo11.html.

Kassin, S. (2005) On the psychology of confessions. *American Psychologist, 60*, 215–28.

Lassiter, G. D. (2004) *Interrogations, confessions and entrapment*. New York: Kluwer.

Milne, R. and Bull, R. (1999) *Investigative interviewing; psychology and practice*. Chichester: Wiley.

Scottish Executive (2004) *Guidance on interviewing child witnesses*. Available at http:/www.Scotland.gov.uk/library5/justice/cwis-02.asp.

Williamson, T. (2006) *Investigative interviewing*. Cullompton, UK: Willan.

detecting deception

A number of books have been published that claim to reveal behavioural cues to lying. Some have focused on the criminal setting and have been based on experienced investigators' beliefs about such cues. Unfortunately, recent criminal psychology research has found much of what such books claim to be signs of deceit to be mistaken. That is, although relevant professionals and lay people in several countries share the same beliefs about supposed cues to lying, these beliefs are largely wrong. In this section we will look first at the beliefs and then at the reality.

beliefs about cues to lying

A recent review of many dozens of studies about behavioural cues to lying reported, as have previous reviews, that people think liars avert their gaze more (i.e. look you in the eye less), move their hands and feet more, shift their body position more, gesture more and touch their own body more. The reason why people think this probably relates to the fact that such behaviours are fairly useful indicators of nervousness. If liars are nervous then they may behave like this.

Many of the beliefs about signs of deceit rest on the assumptions that when people lie they experience emotion and they may have to think about the lies. The problem is that people telling the truth may well do the same. Innocent suspects may become emotional and have to think hard when being questioned by the police, especially if the interviewers are forceful, aggressive or coercive. When one is emotional it is often difficult to remember things, so that even recent experiences are hard to remember. On the other hand, some criminals may not be emotional about their crimes or during police interviews (which they may have experienced many times). They may well also have taken time to prepare and practise their lies so that they come to mind easily.

Given that there seems to be strong agreement among people about which cues they believe would indicate lying, liars will, of course, share in this knowledge. They will therefore try, when lying, not to give off these cues. This is a likely explanation of the surprising yet consistent finding from psychological research that people are usually poor at detecting lying in others.

A recent review of studies of how good people usually are at detecting lies from behavioural cues demonstrated that they are typically little or no better than chance at this. The main reason for this is that when most people lie they do not usually behave in line with other people's beliefs about cues to lying.

So what does research tell us about how people usually behave when lying? A recent overview of many dozens of previous, worldwide studies concluded that there are no perfectly reliable behavioural cues to deception. The previous studies had in total examined over 150 possible cues. The cues that had been examined in several studies did not produce the same effect across the studies. That is, while some studies did find a cue to discriminate to a certain extent between lying and truth-telling, other studies did not. However, relatively few of the studies involved 'high stakes' situations (i.e. the cost of the lies being detected would be high in real life terms). Those that did produced rather few behavioural differences and the strength of the differences was not high.

Most of the research that has just been reviewed above involved lie detectors who were not relevant professionals (e.g. they were students). Perhaps professionals would be better at detecting deception.

how good are professionals at detecting deception from behaviour?

Professor Aldert Vrij of the University of Portsmouth briefly overviewed published research on how good professionals (e.g. police officers) seem to be at detecting deception from behavioural and speech cues, and offered reasons to explain why their performance to date seems far from perfect.

His overview of ten studies of professionals found an average accuracy rate for detecting lies/truths of fifty-five per cent, which is not that different from chance (at fifty per cent) nor from that achieved by non-professionals. In only a few studies have professionals performed better than chance (e.g. sixty-four per cent for USA secret service agents). A major criticism of almost all published studies involving professionals is that the video clips shown to them have not been of people lying in real-life, high stakes situations (but usually of students lying for the purposes of the experiment).

Due to the ever-growing mutual respect between British police forces and criminal psychologists, which a number of psychologists have over the decades worked hard to achieve, we were able to secure comprehensive assistance from a large police force in England to conduct a realistic lie detection study. This involved real-life police interviews with suspects that were video recorded. These recordings were observed for the purposes of our study by a large sample of police officers (not involved in the investigations). We found an average lie/truth accuracy rate of sixty-five per cent (which is significantly better than the chance rate of fifty per cent), with the lie detection rate being sixty-six per cent and truth detection sixty-four per cent. Furthermore, those officers who were more experienced in investigative interviewing performed better. Interestingly, those officers whose beliefs about cues to deception fitted with lay people's stereotypical beliefs (for example, gaze aversion, fidgeting) were the poorest at detecting lies/truths and those who mentioned 'story' cues (e.g. amount of detail, contradictions) were the best. (For more on 'story' cues see the section below on analysing what people say.)

So why are many professionals such as police officers far from perfect at detecting deception? Professor Vrij has suggested a number of reasons that are based on psychological theory and research. First, and perhaps foremost, there are dozens of research studies on how people actually behave when lying, which consistently have revealed that when lying compared to when they are telling the truth some people show increases in certain behaviours, while other people show decreases or no change in the same behaviours. Furthermore, in some lying/truth-telling situations a person's behaviours may increase, but the same person's behaviours may decrease in other deceptive situations. There are several possible reasons for this. One is that when the stakes are higher (as in our study involving real-life police interviews with suspects) emotions may be stronger, thus affecting behaviour more. Another is that many people when lying try hard not to give off the cues they believe people look for in liars (e.g. increases in behaviour), and they either succeed in this or they over-control their behaviour, resulting in decreases. Yet another might relate to whether liars have had time to prepare/practise their lies. When we analysed the behaviour of the police suspects in our study we found lying to be associated not with the cues people commonly believe in (see the above section) but with a decrease in blinking and in hand/arm movements (females) and an increase in speech pauses. A further reason why many professionals seem poor at lie detecting is that they may concentrate their efforts on analysing people's behaviour (especially facial cues – some of which are, in fact, among the easiest for liars to control) rather than on their speech content and on how they say it. Such a focus would seem counterproductive if speech cues are better guides to lying (see the section below). However, if the police conduct interviews with suspects in ways that do not effectively encourage the suspects to speak (see chapter 4), they will produce fewer speech cues. This is one reason why police interviewers who are unprepared and not properly trained may often make lie detection mistakes when interviewing suspects (e.g. letting a guilty person go free).

So how might professionals become better lie detectors? First of all, they need proper training on how to conduct information gathering investigative interviews (see chapter 4). Secondly, they need training (based on the results of relevant, published, quality research rather than on speculation) to avoid relying on the stereotypical but wrong cues (see above), and guidance on which cues can be better guides, with the clear acknowledgement that even these cues are not that reliable as indications of lying. Furthermore, they need training to overcome other false beliefs such as (i) honest or attractive-looking people lie less and (ii) people who look nervous are liars (when they are probably just socially anxious or introverted). Then, they need to understand that if professionals behave in an accusatory or aggressive or suspicious way this in itself may well result in the person giving off cues that the professionals believe to be signs of lying. They also need training to combine useful cues from behaviour and from speech (see the section below on combining lie detection methods). Finally, they need guidance on how to avoid revealing near the beginning of the interview most or all of the information they have about the crime and the suspect (see chapter 4).

training to detect deception from behaviour

A number of books that claim to improve people's ability to detect deception have been published. However, many of the behaviours these books claim to be guides to deception are not valid cues. A small number of better quality research studies have been published in which participants observe video recordings of people that have been analysed for which behaviours best discriminated between their lying and truth-telling. Some of the participants were told which cues actually discriminated and some were not.

The effects of such training have usually been found to be weak. One reason for this could be that people may find it difficult to ignore their own (false) beliefs about which cues indicate lying and therefore they benefit little from the training. Over the decades psychological research has repeatedly found that when people are emotional their range of attention narrows and they are more reliant on their basic, well-established beliefs. Thus if training (as it should) offers them new ideas they may not employ these in emotional/stressful/difficult situations.

A few years ago in the USA one psychological experiment involved training half of a group of students in cues that a book for interrogators claimed were related to deception. The trained group were worse than the untrained group on a subsequent detection deception task!

In one of the better studies on this topic, Canadian parole officers and students received training that involved:

- myth dissolution (information that common beliefs about cues to deception are usually wrong)
- describing the cues that some research studies have found to indicate lying in some people
- feedback on how accurate were their lie detection decisions.

Overall, there was an improvement across the training, but some of this could merely have been due to practice. Nevertheless, this study highlighted the importance of receiving feedback on the accuracy of our lie detection decisions, which is something that professionals rarely receive (e.g. a customs officer questions some individuals, believes them and therefore does not search their bags which do, in fact, contain illegal items). On the other hand, prison inmates may have experienced feedback (e.g. from their judgements of others who might lie often) concerning whether their judgements were correct. This could explain why a study in Sweden found prisoners to be better than chance (i.e. sixty-five vs. fifty per cent) at detecting deception when observing video tapes made at the university of people lying or telling the truth.

detecting deception from speech content

criteria-based content analysis

In Germany in the 1950s the Supreme Court was concerned about relying on information provided (solely) by one or more young children to convict someone of the very serious crime of child sexual abuse. Therefore, it endorsed the idea that relevant experts (who are court appointed in the German inquisitorial criminal justice system) analyse such children's accounts for indications that the children may well be describing genuinely experienced events. This analysis is usually referred to as criteria-based content analysis (CBCA). This analysis is part of 'Statement Validity Assessment', which courts in Germany, Sweden and the Netherlands have been using to guide their decisions. CBCA is based on a number of sensible assumptions, among which are that statements (i.e. the contents of what a person says) derived from memory of actual experiences differ in quality/content from those based on fabrication. Nineteen different criteria can be used to analyse the statements to help decide which are true. These criteria relate to (i) general characteristics of the statement (e.g. the amount of detail), (ii) specific contexts (e.g. reproduction of con-versation, unexpected complications during the incident), (iii) motivation related contents (e.g. the child spontaneously correct-ing herself when giving her statement – something which liars may worry about doing) and (iv) details characteristic of that type of offence (e.g. that the child was 'groomed' before being abused).

However, it was not until many years after this procedure had been used in courts that research was conducted on its accuracy (for more on what constitutes accuracy see this chapter's later section, 'Can a testing procedure be relied upon?'). At a conference in Sweden in the early 1980s one of the 'founding fathers' of SVA/CBCA (Professor Udo Undeutsch) gave an Invited Lecture on this procedure which, for those invited delegates from the UK and the USA, was the first time they had heard in detail about this pro-cedure and that it had already played a role in thousands of German court cases. At the end of his lecture I asked Professor Undeutsch what research had been conducted to assess its accuracy. He said that there had been none, the main reason for this being that, in his opinion, no research study could contain an event and subsequent interviewing that would approximate sexual abuse.

Nevertheless, in the last twenty years over thirty studies have examined CBCA and the general conclusion from them is that such analysis can discriminate between true and untrue accounts at a level above chance (averaging around seventy-two per cent), but not close to perfection. However, the various studies have found different (of the nineteen) criteria to discriminate between truthful and not truthful accounts. Some of these studies have analysed statements not of children (for whom the procedure was originally devised) but of adults (whose maturity could allow them purposely to provide some of the criteria in their false statements). Also, almost all of the studies have not been of real-life (see this chapter's later section on the difficulty in real-life studies of establishing the 'ground' truth, that is whether a statement actually is true). Furthermore, to properly analyse statements using CBCA probably requires a lot of training, which some of the studies did not adequately provide. Even so, the general idea that a reasonable proportion of true statements differ from false statements in terms of their contents may have some merit when examining the statements of liars who are unaware of this idea.

Another approach, called 'reality monitoring', examines the content of what people say.

reality monitoring

This approach to detecting deception is based on the assumption that memories based on experienced events (i.e. external sources) can be differentiated from memories based on imagining, thinking and reasoning (i.e. internal sources). That is, memories for what actually happened (truths) are different to some extent from made up stories (lies). Crucial to this approach is the notion that perceptual processes are very much involved in putting into memory truly experienced events involving information of a contextual (space, time), sensory (shapes, colours) and auditory (speech) nature. Thus true memories should contain such types of information, whereas lies involve many more thought processes (called cognitive operations).

A recent review of all previous studies found that the average accuracy of detecting truth/lies using this reality monitoring (RM) approach was around seventy per cent (when chance is fifty per cent). However, different studies had found different aspects of the RM criteria (i.e. information types) to be the most useful, and have defined the criteria in different ways. Furthermore, the delay between the event and the describing of it seems to affect the extent to which memories based on external sources (i.e. truths) still contain more contextual, sensory and semantic information. All of the studies so far published have been experiments conducted for research purposes (e.g. people lied/told the truth at the request of the experimenter). Real-life field studies are needed.

computer analysis

A recent development in the analysis of speech to detect deception involves the use of computer software to analyse written transcripts of what people say. (These transcripts are written by humans who listen to tape recordings of people lying and telling the truth.) The software allocates each word spoken to a category (e.g. spatial, affective, cognitive) that theoretically may relate to lying/truth-telling in a way similar to the reality monitoring approach (see above). The software can also allocate the words to linguistic categories such as 'negative emotions' and 'first person singular' (e.g. I, me, my). However, at present the software has quite a high error rate (of around twenty per cent – which is not better than trained humans). Nevertheless, a recent study of prisoners lying and telling the truth about what happened in video clips that they had just seen found that these types of automatic computer-based transcript analyses to have a truth/lie detection rate significantly better than chance. However, a few word categories occurred more frequently in the way opposite to that predicted (e.g. more spatial words while lying). Clearly, more research is needed.

A recent study in the USA focused not on direct speech (e.g. one person speaking to another) but on the language used in messages such as e-mails. This pioneering study found that some of the cues were effective (e.g. deceivers displayed less 'lexical diversity', 'content diversity', and more 'modifiers'). Contrary to previous research on direct speech, they found that in e-mail messages it was the deceivers who used more words (especially verbs, noun phrases and sentences). Again, much more research on this new topic is needed. (For more on forensic linguistics see chapter 7.)

combining behavioural and speech cues

One possible way to improve lie detection is to combine the cues that have been found to be better than useless. If one analysed video tapes of people when known to be lying and telling the truth, one could (as described above) discover which cues (at least in those tapes, of those people, in that setting) occurred more (or less) often during the lies than during the truths. One could then analyse those video tapes (using only the valid cues) to see what success rate could be achieved. Professor Vrij did this using video recordings from two of our earlier studies involving nurses and students lying about a recent event.

In one of those studies liars showed fewer illustrators and hand/finger movements, longer response latency and more speech errors/hesitations, they also had a lower total CBCA score and RM score. (However, we must not forget that other studies have not found these behavioural cues to be associated with lying, but have found other cues to discriminate to a certain extent between truth and lies.) When all the cues found in the two studies to discriminate to some extent between truth and lies were combined, the resulting (complex statistical) analysis produced an accuracy rate of eighty-one per cent for the first study, eighty-eight per cent for the second study, and seventy-nine per cent for both studies' data combined. (Note that these percentages are not based on humans making lie detection judgements but on counting up the cues, via video analysis, when the people were (i) lying and (ii) telling the truth.) These percentages indicate what the maximum possible accuracy rate should be (a) if observers reliably used only the cues found in these studies actually to discriminate between lies and truth or (b) if suitable technology could ever be developed to monitor and quantify these cues.

Of course, other people (or the same people) in other situations might show different cues to lying. It is also very important to note that most of the cues employed in this combined approach relate to what people say and how they say it. If police interviews with possible liars are not conducted in a way that results in good samples of speech from the interviewees (see chapter 4), then a combined approach will be able to add little to the much lower detection rates that are typically found from the visual analysis of behaviour.

the polygraph

You may have seen the movie *Meet the Parents*, in which a polygraph test was used in attempting to detect deception.

The set of equipment known as the polygraph (from the Greek *pol'* = 'many' and *graph* = 'to write') measures various sorts of internal bodily activities such as heart rate, blood pressure, respiration and palmar sweating. These activities are displayed on charts or on computer screens. Such equipment is used in many medical and scientific settings. Its use in attempting to detect deception is based on the age-old assumption that lying is accompanied by changes in such internal bodily activities. While the equipment does measure such activities with great accuracy, the big issues for polygraphic lie detection are (i) whether deceivers' bodily activities are reliably different when lying than when truth-telling and (ii) whether such differences do not similarly occur in truth-tellers (e.g. an innocent man being questioned about the murder of his wife with whom he was experiencing severe marital difficulties).

This section on polygraphic lie detection tests will focus on the following topics:

- how to determine if a testing procedure can be relied upon;
- its use in criminal investigations;
- its use in security screening.

can a testing procedure be relied upon?

Psychologists around the world have devoted decades of effort to (a) establishing and publicizing how best to determine if tests can be relied upon and (b) assessing the quality of many thousands of tests. This is vitally important work. Just because a person or organization claims to have developed a useful test does not mean that the test is a good one. Many issues are relevant but the most important ones are reliability and validity.

Within psychology *reliability* refers not to accuracy but to similarity across time or among testers. It is the issue of *validity* that is closest to accuracy.

There are several aspects of reliability:

- 'inter-examiner' reliability which focuses on whether different testers make similar judgements to each other when assessing the same person
- 'test-retest' reliability which focuses on whether when re-tested a person receives a similar judgement as when first tested
- 'inter-item' reliability focuses on, for example, whether the various questions put to the person taking the test lead to the same conclusion.

Validity is concerned with the extent to which a test assesses what it claims to assess. It too has several aspects:

- face validity is the extent to which a test (on the face of it) looks like it assesses what it claims
- content validity is concerned with the relationship of the contents of the test to the phenomenon being assessed
- construct validity concerns the relationship of the test to underlying theories/constructs concerning the phenomenon

- criterion validity is the extent to which scores on the test actually predict outcomes (e.g. how accurate the procedure is at classifying people as lying or truth-telling)
- incremental validity concerns how well a test compares with other tests that have been designed to examine the same phenomenon (e.g. detecting deceit).

All of the above forms of reliability and validity are crucially important in determining whether a testing procedure (such as polygraphic lie detection) actually is effective. Let us now look at research on whether polygraphic lie detection has been found to be accurate in the criminal setting.

the use of the polygraph in criminal investigations

In the early days of attempting to detect criminal lying with a procedure involving the polygraph, a number of questioning techniques were developed, some of which have now been largely abandoned. For example, the relevant-irrelevant technique which compares physiological reactions to questions relevant to the crime with those not relevant. One of the major problems with this technique was that some innocent people (e.g. a loving husband) reacted strongest to relevant questions (e.g. 'Did you murder your wife?'). Nowadays, one of two questioning techniques are usually employed, these being the Control Question Test and the Guilty Knowledge Test.

The Control Question Test (CQT) compares reactions to questions about the topic being investigated with reactions to questions that are thought to be arousing and that both guilty and innocent people will lie to. This procedure is based on the assumption that for an innocent person the latter type of questions will cause the greater reactions but that for a guilty person (who will be lying to all questions) the former type of questions will occasion larger reactions. Among the problems with the CQT is that innocent people may still react more strongly to the crime-relevant questions, especially if they fear that their answers to these will not be believed. Also, innocent people taking a polygraph test would be aware that if reliable information supporting their innocence were available, they would not need to take a polygraph test. Therefore, they know that it is difficult to prove their innocence and thus they are very concerned about the crime-relevant questions. This is probably why the CQT (for more on this see below) is not that good at correctly classifying innocent persons.

The Guilty Knowledge Test (GKT) compares reactions to various items, some of which may reveal knowledge of the crime. For example, the polygraph examiner may show a murder suspect several types of handgun, one of which is identical to the one used in the shooting. The suspect will be asked separately for each gun whether he or she recognizes it (or have ever touched it). This procedure is based on the assumption that the polygraphic reactions for guilty persons will be greater for the gun used in the shooting. So long as the alternatives (e.g. the various types of gun) are sufficiently similar to each other so that the 'correct' one does not stand out to an innocent suspect and the media or the police have not let slip (to the innocent suspect) what the 'correct' alternative is, then the GKT may not suffer as a procedure from as many problems at the CQT. However, as we shall see when we overview research studies of the GKT and the CQT, the former does at times seem to fail to correctly classify guilty people.

Most of the published research on the accuracy of use of the polygraph to detect deception has been focused on the criminal setting, but the vast majority of this research has not involved real crimes or real criminals. This is for a variety of reasons, including knowing the 'ground truth'.

Ground truth involves knowing (independently, of course, of the polygraph testing procedure) whether the person being tested is lying or not. In real life (e.g. in police investigations) it is extremely difficult to be certain what took place during a crime and who was involved. A police suspect may be happy to admit that he or she was present but deny wrongdoing (e.g. state that sexual intercourse occurred by consent not rape). Unless there is rock-solid evidence that the person being tested is lying or truth-telling, the validity of the polygraph procedure cannot be properly assessed. Of course, if there is such rock-solid evidence, a polygraph lie-detection test may well be superfluous.

Because ground truth is so difficult to assess in real-life investigations, the majority of the published studies that have tried to assess the effectiveness of the polygraph in criminal investigations have had to employ 'mock' crime scenarios.

laboratory studies

A recent review of the possible effectiveness of the polygraph in mock crimes in the laboratory settings was provided by Professor Charles Honts. He noted for the CQT that once 'inconclusive' decisions had been removed from the data set the accuracy rate for 'guilty' persons (i.e. liars) was ninety-one per cent and for 'innocent' persons eighty-nine per cent. However, even though some researchers have shown ingenuity in designing their laboratory studies to have some aspects similar to real-life criminal investigations, for ethical (and other) reasons it is probably the case that laboratory studies will never be very similar to real life (e.g. the fear experienced by an innocent person accused of murder who knows he had a motive and was alone at the time of the killing).

field studies

Because ground truth is so difficult to determine, relatively few 'field' (i.e. 'real life') studies of the effectiveness of polygraphic lie detection have been published. The 2004 report of the British Psychological Society (BPS) overviewed previously published reviews of such field studies, noting that determining ground truth via confessions (for example) is problematic because such confessions may have been, in part, affected by polygraph outcomes (e.g. a guilty person who passes the test may decide not to confess).

The majority of these field studies have employed the CQT – explained above. The BPS report (2004) noted on page 15 that 'There is reasonable agreement between the reviews regarding guilty suspects. Correct classifications were made in 83 per cent to 89 per cent of the cases, whereas incorrect decisions (classifying a guilty suspect as innocent) were made in 10 per cent to 17 per cent of the cases.' However, with regard to innocent suspects the report noted that these 'are less encouraging. ... Depending on the review, between fifty-three per cent and seventy-eight per cent of innocent suspects were correctly classified and between eleven per cent and forty-seven per cent were incorrectly classified' (p.15). (The review with the lowest rate of incorrect classifications of innocent suspects had the highest 'inconclusive' rate of twenty-nine per cent). Thus, as with laboratory mock studies using the CQT, while the error rate for incorrectly classifying guilty people is low, that for incorrectly classifying innocent people (i.e. as liars) is higher.

A few field studies have employed the Guilty Knowledge Test (GKT). The BPS report noted that these found high accuracy for classifying innocent suspects (ninety-four to ninety-eight per cent) but rather low accuracy for guilty suspects (forty-two to seventy-six per cent). This mirrors the outcomes of laboratory/mock studies using the GKT. While its error rate for incorrectly classifying innocent people is low, that for incorrectly classifying guilty people (i.e. failing to detect liars) is higher.

Thus, the test/approach that has the stronger theoretical basis (the GKT) is the one that seems poorest at detecting the very people it was designed to detect (i.e. those with guilty knowledge). One reason for this is that guilty people, rather than innocent people, will be motivated to beat the test by the employment of what is referred to as countermeasures. These deliberate attempts may involve:

- attempting to lessen physiological activity (i.e. what the polygraph measures) in response to relevant questions (CQT) or items (GKT).
- attempting to increase such activity in response to irrelevant questions or items.

The latter usually is easier to achieve than the former, unless one is well trained.

Many professional polygraphers claim that they believe they can detect the use of countermeasures. However, the quality published studies on this have shown that the use of countermeasures can be very effective.

use of the polygraph in security screening

Another problem with regard to the test error rates (mentioned above) relates to the number of innocent suspects caught up in an investigation. Some countries are believed to employ polygraph testing to help determine who within, or wishing to join, their security services is a threat (e.g. a spy or a terrorist). They do this by testing a large number of people among whom few, if any, are a serious threat. In the USA the National Research Council (2003) pointed out that if, for example, the frequency of serious threat in an organization such as the security services is ten in ten thousand and a test procedure needs to detect at least eighty per cent of these threats, then over 1,600 people would fail the test. On the other hand, given that it is usually a considerable problem to mis-classify innocent people (e.g. worthy employees) as threats, to have a much lower number of 'false alarms' (say about forty) would require setting a high degree of difference between truth-telling physiological activity and lying physiological activity which would result in eight of the ten threats passing the test.

The inevitable weaknesses that exist in polygraphic lie detection led the National Research Council and the British Psychological Society to review the effectiveness of other possible methods to detect deception.

We mentioned above that in some countries the polygraph is used to test whether people who wish or are recommended to join the security services are telling the truth when being questioned about their intentions and their past. In a few countries some non-security organizations still, probably mistakenly, use polygraph testing to select employees even though after a review of the relevant research and human rights arguments the government of the USA in 1988 brought in the Polygraph Protection Act which prohibits the use of polygraph testing for employee selection (except by some government security agencies and in some strategic industries such as nuclear power).

Given that use of polygraph testing in pre-employment screening is beset by a number of problems, what can psychology offer? The BPS report overviews some other ways of assessing people's honesty and integrity, for example voice stress analysis.

voice stress analysis

In this chapter's earlier section on observing behaviour we noted that some research studies have found that certain aspects of speaking (e.g. increases in voice pitch and speech errors) may be related (in some people, in some situations) to lying. While such increases in voice pitch may be small and hard to detect with the human ear, equipment has been designed that can accurately note such changes in pitch. Such equipment, often referred to as 'voice stress analysers', has been used in attempts to detect lying (though few studies on this have been published). For example, some insurance companies have been rumoured to be using voice stress analysers when people telephone to make a claim (e.g. that items were stolen while they were on holiday). The problems limiting the accuracy of such procedures are very similar to those for polygraph testing (e.g. truthful people may be stressed and therefore their voice pitch rises and skilled liars may not be stressed).

In its overview the National Research Council (2003) concluded that 'The practical performance of voice stress analysis for detecting deception has not been impressive' (p.168) and that there is 'little or no scientific basis for the use of ... voice measurement instruments as an alternative to the polygraph' (p.168). However, whereas the polygraph usually requires the person being tested to be connected to the apparatus, voice stress analysis does not. This might result in fewer innocent/truthful people being stressed by the procedure, but it does raise issues of human rights (e.g. being aware that one is being tested). (Some new types of polygraph testing which monitor physiological activity without the person being aware of it may be under development.)

conclusions

Each of the methods and procedures used to try to detect deception has its severe limitations, many of which are inherent and therefore can never be overcome. Each seems to have error rates that are far from negligible. Even with training and experience (plus the most up-to-date equipment) people are typically far from perfect at catching liars. There is probably a very good reason for this. Humans have spent many thousands of years learning to deceive others. It would be naive of us, therefore, to think that lie detection will ever achieve very high accuracy rates. The 2004 BPS report said, 'We must not deceive ourselves into thinking that there will ever be an error-free way of detecting deception' (p. 30).

recommended further reading

British Psychological Society (2004) *A review of the current scientific status and fields of application of polygraphic deception detection.* Leicester: BPS. Available from http://www.bps.org/publications; click on 'Working Party Reports'.

DePaulo, B., Lindsay, J., Malone, B., Muhlenbruck, L., Charlton, K. and Cooper, H. (2003) Cues to deception. *Psychological Bulletin, 129,* 74–118.

Granhag, P. A. and Stromwall, L. (2004) *The detection of deception in forensic contexts.* Cambridge: Cambridge University Press.

Hartwig, M., Granhag, P. A., Stromwall, I. and Andersson, L. (2004) Suspicious minds: Criminals' ability to detect deception. *Psychology, Crime and Law, 10,* 83–95.

Masip, J., Sporer, S., Garrido, E. and Herrero, C. (2005) The detection of deception with the reality monitoring approach: A review of the empirical evidence. *Psychology, Crime and Law, 11,* 99–122.

Memon, A., Vrij, A. and Bull, R. (2003) *Psychology and law: Truthfulness, accuracy and credibility,* 2nd edn. Chichester: Wiley.

National Research Council (2003) *The polygraph and lie detection.* Committee to Review the Scientific Evidence on the Polygraph. Washington, DC: The National Academic Press.

Vrij, A. (2000) *Detecting lies and deceit.* Chichester: Wiley.

Vrij, A. (2004) Why professionals fail to catch liars and how they can improve. *Legal and Criminological Psychology, 9,* 159–81.

eyewitness testimony

In 2004 the author of this chapter was contacted by a solicitor (i.e. a legal representative) in Scotland whose client was accused of a serious crime. The evidence against the client involved eyewitnesses. The solicitor requested a written report on several psychological factors that he considered relevant to the eyewitnesses' evidence. Among these factors were the possible effects of (i) the consumption of a large amount of alcohol on witness perception and memory, (ii) being shown a photograph of a person on a later attempt to try to identify the perpetrator at an identification parade/line-up, (iii) the client being the only person in the line-up whose facial hair colour matched the witness' original description and (iv) whether asking a witness during a trial if the perpetrator is present in court adds anything to the earlier identification (i.e. made at the line-up). The report led, in 2005, to its author being required to be at the court building during the defence part of the trial in case he was called to testify (i.e. in front of judge and jury).

In the UK it is relatively rare for psychologists to testify (as expert witnesses) in criminal trials on factors that may influence the reliability of witness testimony. The major reason for this has been the traditional view of trial judges that what criminal psychology research has found out is already within the common knowledge of jurors and therefore that expert testimony on such matters is not required (the role of expert witnesses being to assist the court). In recent years in England the views of some judges has changed to some extent and they will allow expert witness testimony if this testimony is likely to inform jurors of matters of which they are likely to be unaware (so long as the expert testimony is based on reliable information such as quality research that has been published). In some countries, for example the USA, the rules about the admissibility of expert witness testimony, how qualified/experienced such experts need to be and the research on which their testimony is based should be published are different from in the UK.

However, in Scotland it seems that in criminal trials very few psychologists had ever been allowed to testify on factors that could influence eyewitness testimony. Thus the author of this chapter was reticent about travelling the hundreds of miles to Scotland only for it to be decided that he would not be allowed to testify as an expert witness. To his surprise, he was allowed to testify on the four factors mentioned above.

In 1974 the Government in England and Wales asked an eminent judge to chair a committee of inquiry to produce a report that would try to explain why honest witnesses can give mistaken testimony (e.g. identify the wrong person as being the crime perpetrator). The committee was set up in response to a number of factors including media focus on people who had been found guilty and put in jail based on witness testimony that was later shown to be mistaken. This committee's report (known as the Devlin Report after its chairman) was published in 1976 and it called for more psychological insight and research to be provided on this topic, since rather little was available at that time. In response to this the author of this chapter invited a colleague (Brian Clifford) to join him in writing a book (published in 1978) entitled *The Psychology of Person Identification* which overviewed the various insights that psychological findings and theories were then able to offer. In the decades since then many thousands of research papers and dozens of books have been published on the topic. In England and Wales the many pupils who now choose psychology as one of the three or so specialist subjects they study in the last two years of school or college will cover the topic of eyewitness testimony, which has now become one of the major topics, worldwide, in psychology.

In the USA from the mid 1990s the Innocence Project (see the Recommended Further Reading list at the end of this chapter for the address of its web site) has found that many falsely convicted and imprisoned people were there based on honest but mistaken eyewitness testimony. The Project often proved that the convictions were false by very modern use of DNA testing (a procedure pioneered by Sir Alec Jeffreys here at the University of Leicester). In response The Attorney General of the United States set up a committee to produce guidelines for the police relating to the obtaining of eyewitness evidence. Some of the kinds of psychological research that informed these guidelines will be described in this chapter.

Some recent psychological research studies of witnesses to real-life crimes have confirmed the concern shown by the 1970s Government committee of enquiry and by the Innocence Project. For example, in Sweden a 2005 study examined the descriptions given to the police by twenty-nine witnesses who saw the assassination of the Foreign Minister (Anna Lindh). The accuracy of their descriptions of the perpetrator was gauged from comparison with the appearance of the assassin on a video-recording from a surveillance camera a few minutes before the killing. The witnesses' descriptions of age, height and body build were largely inaccurate. (However, this study involved only one criminal who could have been particularly difficult to describe.)

A 2004 study in Norway compared security camera video-recordings of robberies at banks and post offices with witnesses' descriptions of the perpetrators. It found that forty-four per cent of the height descriptions were 'accurate' and a further thirty-four per cent were 'partly accurate' but that forty per cent of the age descriptions were 'incorrect'. (However, it should be noted that all the robbers had covered their faces in one way or another.) This study further found that witnesses who gave fuller descriptions were not more accurate. A study in the Netherlands that compared witness descriptions to those convicted of robberies also found that witnesses to these real-life crimes who gave fuller descriptions were not more accurate. It found that these descriptions contained largely rather general descriptors (e.g. 'tall') and few identifying details. In England a 2003 study of witnesses' performance at real life identification parades/line-ups found that those who had provided more detailed descriptions to the police were more likely to pick out the suspect but the extent to which their descriptions actually matched the suspect was not related to whether the suspect was picked out or not.

Psychological research on factors that may influence witness testimony has actually been conducted for over eighty years. This research has tended to focus on (i) aspects of the witnesses (e.g. alcohol consumption), (ii) aspects of the crime (e.g. weapon usage) and (iii) aspects of the police investigation (e.g. whether a photograph of a man was shown to the witness some days before they saw him in a line-up). The third of these aspects can be improved in the light of psychological research but the first two usually cannot. Nevertheless, research on these aspects can inform decisions as to whether witness evidence can be relied upon.

The most crucial contribution of criminal psychology to better evaluation of eyewitness testimony has been to try to make investigators, courts, and juries aware that memory does not act like a tape recorder. Thousands of psychological research studies have found that (i) during an event we can only focus on certain parts of it, (ii) we do not put all these parts into memory and (iii) when we try to retrieve from memory the (limited amount of) information that actually is in there about the event we (a) cannot retrieve all that is there and (b) we 'add' to what is retrieved based on our expectations.

aspects of witnesses

Much of the research on aspects of witnesses has found that these have little effect on performance (e.g. whether the witness was female or male, a member of the public or a police officer, confident or not, intelligent). These are important findings. For example, jurors or judges might mistakenly think that a confident witness should be relied on more than a non-confident witness.

However, a topic that only recently has begun to receive the attention of criminal psychologists is that of elderly witnesses. Research has found that people over the age of sixty-five years make more mistakes than younger adults when trying to pick out from a set of photographs the person they saw previously committing a (mock) crime. This seems especially so when the set of photographs does not, in fact, contain the perpetrator (but similar people to him, as required by police 'regulations' in several countries). This is not due to poor vision but may well be due, research results suggest, to elderly witnesses having difficulty remembering (and/or grasping the reason for) the instruction (required to be given by the police in England) that the perpetrator 'may or may not be' among the photographs. Research has also found that young children will choose someone from a photospread when the originally seen face is not there.

Another aspect of witnesses that some research has found to be important is whether they are familiar with the nature of the appearance of the perpetrator. For example, if the perpetrators were from a part of the world with which the witness was not familiar, the witness may have greater difficulty in (i) describing them and (ii) picking them out from a set of similar-looking people (e.g. in a set of photographs or in a line-up). There is now quite an extensive research literature available on what is termed 'cross-racial' identification (though this phrase is rather inappropriate). Such research has often, but not always, found that people are better at identifying faces of 'types' they have extensive experience of than types they have limited or no experience of. (However, in many of these laboratory based studies the participants initially have been shown many faces, each very briefly, to later recognize among an even larger set rather than initially just one or two faces, as in most crimes, to later identify from several.) One of the current leading psychological explanations of these findings is that people are able to encode (i.e. put into memory) more information concerning the types of faces they are familiar with. An interesting point that arises from research on this topic is that, if it is indeed more difficult for witnesses to successfully identify a person from a different 'type', then such an identification, if correct, should carry more weight (e.g. in court).

Another important aspect of humans that psychology has studied is their expectations about the type of person who would commit crime. For example, we expect bad things to have been committed by nasty people and good things by attractive people. A seminal experiment conducted in Scotland illustrates this well. Members of the public were provided, by the psychologists, with experience of seeing a face and later trying (from memory) to reconstruct a likeness of it using sets of photographs of eyes, noses, chins and so on. Then these participants were (unknown to them) all shown the same face but half of them were led to believe it was of a murderer whereas the other half were led to believe it was a lifeboat man. Their facial reconstructions were shown to other participants (who knew no details of the experiment). This second group of participants were each shown one of the reconstructions and were asked to rate the 'person' on a number of personality characteristics. Those who were shown reconstructions made by people who were led to believe that the original face was of a murderer rated him as more dishonest and more unattractive than did those shown the reconstructions made by people who were led to believe that the original face was of a lifeboat man.

Criminal psychology research has also found that the general public share ideas of what certain types of criminal look like (e.g. drug dealer, company fraudster). However, these commonsense beliefs may not be valid or reliable.

aspects of the crime

Much of the psychological research relating to aspects of the crime has produced findings that do support commonsense (e.g. the effects of poor street lighting). One of the topics where the research findings differ from surveys of common sense beliefs is that concerning the effects of levels of violence. Many people assume that the more violent the event the more memorable it will be. A growing number of research studies have scientifically examined the effects on witness testimony of emotion/stress/arousal or of the presence of a weapon.

Most psychological research experiments on the effects of strong emotion or of stress or fear have found that witness memory is restricted to the more 'central' parts of the event so that while witness testimony for some aspects of the event could be enhanced, memory for other (i.e. less central) aspects is poorer. This may well be partly due to where the witness focuses attention. However, in experiments it is extremely difficult to engender strong emotion or fear due to ethical reasons.

While I was writing this chapter, the media in the UK and around the world were publicizing the fact that an innocent Brazilian man was shot dead on the London underground railway in the police hunt for the people who had bombed this passenger railway some days earlier. After the shooting the first media reports included witness information (e.g. about his behaviour and outer clothing) that suggested that he could have been a bomber. However, some days later it became known that his clothing was not 'bulky' (possibly concealing a suicide bomb) nor did he leap the ticket barrier while being pursued by the police.

The police were very alert to the possibility of suicide bombing and their stress/emotion/arousal may have caused them to ignore (non-central) cues that could have indicated that the man they were following was the wrong one. (They appeared to have followed him from a residential building where a suspected bomber was thought to be staying.) Furthermore, the act of following a suspected bomber will have increased police arousal and this increased arousal would have combined with the fear of the (possible) bomb. Research we conducted in the late 1990s at the University of Portsmouth (with the help of police firearms officers) examined the effects on shooting behaviour of arousing events in the preceding minutes. Earlier research had found that armed police officers (like other humans) can mis-attribute arousal caused by preceding events as being caused by the (possibly armed) man and therefore shoot him when he, in fact, was not armed.

A considerable number of psychological experiments have studied the so-called 'weapon focus' effect. Among the first experiments were rather straightforward ones which showed, for example, that during the witnessed event people who saw a man getting out a gun from his pocket looked for longer at this item (and therefore less at the man) than did people who saw the same event but with the man getting out a cheque book. The people who saw the gun also were able to remember less about the whole event. Recent studies have been more complex. For example, the author of this chapter was asked to assist the editor of a research journal to decide whether an article (and the research study it described) was good enough for publication. The article was on weapon focus and in its research study some of the witnesses to the (staged) event saw a man get out a gun and some did not. Some of the witnesses saw the man get out part of a frozen chicken, which may seem very odd until one realizes that the researchers had designed their experiment to see if it was the unusualness/ unexpectedness of the object (i.e. chicken, gun) rather than it being a weapon that had affected the witnesses. Other similar studies (e.g. using a stalk of celery) seem to have confirmed that what some call the weapon focus-effect is not restricted to weapons.

One of our studies found that among witnesses who had experience with guns, the more frequent the experience (i.e. as members of the Territorial Army) the less was there a weapon focus effect. In another of our studies thousands of police case files were examined to find the several hundred in which real-life witnesses had been shown by the police identification parades/line-ups that included the suspect plus several other people of similar appearance. In several dozens of these cases a weapon was involved in the crime that had been witnessed. The data analysis found that witness line-up performance was not poorer when a weapon had been involved.

This rare, real-life study casts doubt on the notion that when a crime involves a weapon witnesses/victims focus too much of their attention on it (and/or get over aroused) to the detriment of memorizing what the criminal looked like. On the other hand, the presence of a weapon might subsequently have caused such real life witnesses to be, for example, more motivated and/or more careful at the line-ups than the non-weapon witnesses. This lack of clarity concerning the effects of something (i.e. a weapon) is typical of the many issues that psychology tries to explain. Human beings are very complex and adaptable and therefore it is really not surprising to find that although something like a weapon or stress/arousal may impair one aspect of our psychological activity it may also enhance other aspects. This complexity issue also applies to aspects of the investigation.

aspects of the investigation

Much of the eyewitness research conducted by psychologists has focused on making identification procedures as fair as possible (to the suspect/the accused). This involves reducing the likelihood of false identifications while enabling correct identifications to occur.

One very relevant issue is how witnesses are questioned/interviewed, which was covered in chapter 4. Here, we will focus on assisting witnesses/victims to identify the perpetrator by face or by voice. In many countries, but not yet all, it is now recognized that showing a witness just one face (e.g. using a photograph or the actual suspect him/herself – the latter is called a 'show-up') and asking if this is the perpetrator is not a good procedure. To be of any real value, the witness should be shown several similar-looking people with no undue guidance as to which person to choose. This kind of procedure has become standard police practice in several countries (it has been mandated by law in England and Wales for twenty years) and is strongly recommended in the USA in the 1999 Attorney General's Guidelines (which were informed by the research of psychologists).

However, even with good procedures in place witnesses still make identification errors. With regard to identification parades/line-ups, these can be of four major types which are either (i) in a parade that does actually contain the perpetrator, (a) choosing the wrong person or (b) not choosing anyone, or (ii) in a parade that happens not to contain the actual perpetrator, (c) choosing the innocent suspect or (d) choosing one of the other people present (that are usually in psychology referred to as 'foils' or 'distractors'). Most of the relevant psychological research has focused on developing fair procedures designed to reduce the frequency of error type (a).

Another aspect of criminal investigations that psychological research has examined to try to reduce errors is that involving hypnosis. Many people have an inadequate appreciation of what hypnosis actually involves and what its limitations are. More than fifty years ago some police forces (e.g. in the USA) began to use hypnosis in attempts to assist witnesses recall more of what they had experienced. At that time both police officers and the general public believed that memory was like a movie film and that what investigators needed to do was to help the witness to access such a memory. (As described earlier in this chapter, psychological research has demonstrated such a belief to be inadequate.) In their praiseworthy pursuit of evidence in very serious and difficult to solve cases some police officers found that witnesses who were hypnotized then recalled information about the crime that they had not previously recalled. Indeed, some of this extra recall turned out to be correct and so the police concluded that it was due to the hypnosis, ignoring the possibility that it could have been due to other factors necessary for hypnosis (e.g. a quiet, uninterrupted room and a relaxed, focused witness).

Later research has demonstrated that when people are hypno-tized they may well be more suggestible (e.g. go along with leading or suggestive questions): nowadays police use of hypnosis is relatively rare. Most criminal psychologists now seem to be of the opinion that 'evidence' obtained under hypnosis should not be allowed in court.

A further aspect of witness evidence that psychological research has demonstrated to be error prone is that of voice iden-tification (sometimes referred to as earwitness testimony).

earwitness testimony

In many crimes the perpetrators speak and therefore might later be identified by earwitnesses. Furthermore, in some crimes witnesses may not be able to see the perpetrators but can hear their voices. Thus work by criminal psychologists on voice identification is important.

the value of voice identification evidence

In the early 1980s Brian Clifford and I conducted a programme of research studies for the Government that was given an impetus by the publication of the Devlin Report mentioned earlier in this chapter. The Devlin Committee, which reported to the Home Secretary in 1976, stated that as far as its members were concerned no research had been conducted on voice identification but that 'research should proceed as rapidly as possible into the practicality of voice parades ... or any other appropriate methods'. In a 1984 book chapter in which we reviewed our research (and that of others) we concluded that:

> Until future, more realistic studies argue to the contrary we would recommend that prosecutions based solely on a witness' identification of a suspect's voice (if the suspect is a stranger) ought not to proceed, or if they do proceed they should fail. We say this because, even though the topic of ear-witnessing presently lacks any theoretical underpinnings, we are of the opinion that ear-witnessing and eyewitnessing are similarly and considerably error prone. This is not to say that voice identification should not be used as an aid to the prosecution or the defence, but it should not form any major part of the evidence presented in court.
>
> (This statement was in line with the Devlin Committee's
view on the value of visual identification/
eyewitness evidence.)

Five years later, in 1989, an overview on earwitness identification written by several respected North American psychologists (Deffenbacher *et al.* 1989) examined all the published research on the accuracy with which people (in experiments) are able correctly to identify a voice they heard previously. In their con-cluding paragraph they stated:

> Inasmuch as the results we have reported are optimal in that wit-nesses were not stressed and there was no attempt at voice dis-guise, recognition accuracy at realistic delays and speech sample durations was so low that we would agree with Bull and Clifford's (1984) conclusions. Depending on the parameters involved, recognition of an unfamiliar voice may have a sufficient prob-ability of accuracy that it could be of use in a police investigation. Unless further more ecologically valid studies argue to the con-trary, however, ear-witnessing is so error prone as to suggest that no case should be prosecuted solely on identification evidence involving an unfamiliar voice.

A later overview of research on voice identification was published in 1995. In that chapter a Canadian professor of psychology reviewed not only twelve publications of his own but also some twenty-two publications by other people on the topic of voice identification. The overview stated that 'One of the myths still held by many laypersons and officials in the criminal justice system is the belief that eyewitness memory, including voice recognition, is merely common knowledge' and that 'Most voice identification issues of concern to the court, of course, are for voices of strangers ... identification for unfamiliar voices must by treated with caution.'

Thus research by psychologists (and others) seemed to have established that it would be unwise, in the criminal setting, to rely solely on ear-witness evidence.

In December 1998 the author of this chapter was invited by the British Academy of Forensic Sciences to present a paper on earwitness testimony. In August 1999 the national Court of Appeal (in the case of *Roberts*) reported in its written judgement that the lawyers for the appellant (i.e. the convicted man who was appealing the conviction) had placed before it that 1998 paper and the court noted that among the points made were the following:

- voice identification is more difficult than visual identification;
- voice identification of a stranger's voice is a very difficult task, even where the opportunities to listen to the voice are relatively good;
- voice identification is more likely than visual identification to be wrong;
- ordinary people seem as willing to rely on identification by earwitnesses as they are on identification by eyewitnesses;
- in the light of the above points, the warning given to jurors of the danger of a miscarriage of justice in relation to witnesses who are identifying by voice should be even more stringent than that given to jurors in relation to the evidence of eyewitnesses. It should be brought home to jurors that there is an even greater danger of the earwitnesses believing themselves to be right and yet, in fact, being mistaken;
- earwitness identification is so prone to error that it should not be relied upon for a conviction unless some other supporting or confirming evidence is available.

In the light of these points the Court of Appeal decided, in the particular case before it, that 'We do not think that the identification, which rested almost wholly on the voice of the appellant as he spoke to the police officers, was good enough to enable us to say that this conviction was safe and consequently we quash this conviction.'

In some criminal trials judges do not agree with requests from the defence lawyers that earwitness evidence may be so error-prone that such evidence should not be allowed to form part of the prosecution case. Instead, they sometimes allow an expert witness (such as myself) to testify (e.g. inform the jury) (i) about research findings on the general reliability of earwitnessing (such as that mentioned above) and (ii) on factors directly relevant to the ear-witness evidence being presented in that particular trial. Regarding the latter I have, for example, conducted experiments for and testified in different trials concerning

- whether people could tell which one (the suspect's) of several voices in the 'voice parade' played by the police to the rape victim was the only one that was an edited voice sample (from a police interview), the others speaking in a monologue;

- whether people could tell which voice (again of a suspect) was the only one not reading from a script;
- the extent to which the suspect's voice stood out from the other voices as better matching the voice description given by the witness of the perpetrator's voice (e.g. in terms of having 'an Irish accent' or in another case being 'high pitched').

conclusions

The main impetus for criminal psychologists to address the issue of witness testimony has come from concerns about false convictions. However, it must be noted that the frailties of the human mind also mean that the real perpetrators of crime may not be apprehended unless the police improve their procedures in accord with the findings of relevant psychological research. Thousands of research studies have now been published but in relatively few countries have the police updated their identification procedures and/or governments updated their regulations to take full account of what psychology has discovered to assist in the conviction of the guilty.

recommended further reading

Ainsworth, P. (1998) *Psychology, law and eyewitness testimony.* Chichester: Wiley.

Barton, J., Vrij, A. and Bull, R. (2000) High speed driving: Police use of lethal force during simulated incidents. *Legal and Criminological Psychology,* 5,107–21.

Bull, R. and Clifford, B. (1999) Earwitness testimony. In A. Heaton-Armstrong, E. Shepherd and D. Wolchover (eds) *Witness testimony: Psychological, investigative and evidential perspectives,* pp.194–206. London: Blackstone.

Memon, A., Vrij, A. and Bull, R. (2003) *Psychology and law: Truthfulness, accuracy and credibility,* 2nd edn. Chichester: Wiley.

Wagstaff, G., MacVeigh, J., Boston, R., Scott, L., Brunas-Wagstaff, J. and Cole, J. (2003) Can laboratory findings on eyewitness testimony be generalized to the real world? An archival analysis of the influence of violence, weapon presence, and age on eyewitness accuracy. *Journal of Psychology, 137,* 17–29.

Westcott, H., Davies, G. and Bull, R. (2002) *Children's testimony.* Chichester: Wiley.

Yarmey, A. D. (1995) Earwitness and evidence obtained by other senses. In R. Bull and D. Carson (eds) *Handbook of psychology in legal contexts,* pp. 261–76. Chichester: Wiley.

Yarmey, A. D. (2003) Eyewitnesses. In D. Carson and R. Bull (eds) *Handbook of psychology in legal contexts,* 2nd edn, pp. 533–58. Chichester: Wiley.

online resources

http://www.Innocenceproject.org
The Innocence Project web site.

forensic linguistics

introduction

Compared with forensic psychology, forensic linguistics is a newer and smaller discipline. Forensic linguists share many areas of interest with forensic psychologists and the two disciplines are likely to become increasingly entwined. The purpose of this chapter is to survey some of the areas of forensic linguistics, demonstrate where the two disciplines overlap and highlight some areas of forensic linguistics where forensic psychologists have yet to make a contribution.

Consider the following situation:

> You are on holiday abroad eating in a restaurant. You speak the language a little and are getting by; you know a little of the vocabulary and some useful phrases; you know how to say please and thank you. With your phrasebook and a lot of sign language you are having a good vacation. At the next table there is a group of young men talking and arguing and laughing. They gradually become louder and more animated to the obvious consternation of the staff in the restaurant. Finally two of the men stand up angrily and start throwing punches. One of them falls into your

table and as you push him away he trips over and is hurt. Two policemen arrive and it is obvious that they want to speak with you. You understand that they want to take you somewhere. You try to explain the situation but can't make yourself understood. You don't know quite what is happening and you don't know your rights in this country. One of the policemen says something to you in a slightly 'sing-song' voice. It is clear that what he is saying he has said many times on other days. He is not listening to the meaning of his words and the full meaning is difficult to catch. You gather that essentially they want you to tell them what happened but also you don't have to. There is a question about whether you've understood. You nod uncertainly. You have been read your rights.

Now turn the tables. Someone with limited English finds himself/herself in a similar situation in your local restaurant. The police may decide that the person should be arrested and at this point the law is clear that the person has to be informed of his or her rights. In the first instance this information will be given verbally by the police officer. The caution for the UK is

'You do not have to say anything. But it may harm your defence if you do not mention when questioned something you later rely on in court. Anything you do say may be given in evidence.'

In the United States the equivalent right to be read a caution is called a person's Miranda rights (after the court case which established them). The wording of Miranda rights varies slightly from state to state but the minimal Miranda warning, as outlined in the *Miranda* v. *Arizona* case is given below.

You have the right to remain silent. Anything you say can and will be used against you in a court of law. You have the right to speak to an attorney, and to have an attorney present during any questioning. If you cannot afford a lawyer, one will be provided for you at government expense.

The purpose of the caution is to tell arrested individuals just what their rights are under the law, but the language used to express these rights is not straightforward. Even if English is your first language your rights may not be easy to understand. At a stressful time you need to understand what has been said to you and apply it to your situation. For example, in the case described above if the police officer asks you what happened, should you answer straightaway? Would it be better to stay quiet until you have spoken with a lawyer? What would be the best thing to do? These questions obviously involve points of law but they also involve issues of comprehension.

Any rights under the law have to be communicated through language. What makes the language of the law easy or difficult to understand is one of the topic areas in forensic linguistics. From this understanding forensic linguists can suggest reforms to legal language to make it easier to understand. Whilst this area of forensic linguistics does not have a direct parallel in forensic psychology, in other areas there are overlaps in topics and approaches. Linguists, for example, can use their expertise in language practices to examine the peculiar language that is used in the courtroom. Language reveals lot about the relationships between people and analysis of it can throw light on, for example, power relationships within a courtroom setting.

Forensic linguistics, however, does not restrict itself to understanding the language of the judicial process. Occasionally linguists may be involved in giving evidence in the courtroom. In the example of whether a caution was understood, a linguist might argue that without an interpreter the person's rights were violated and any conviction would thus be unsafe. Two other areas in which linguists might give expert evidence include questions of identification and questions of meaning and use. Identification questions might concern either spoken language using voice analysis or written language. If you received a telephone threat or an abusive letter a forensic linguist might be able to help identify who was behind them. With regard to disputes of meaning, usually these fall to lawyers to debate, but sometimes a linguist can assist. In one case Jerry McMenamin, a Californian forensic linguist, examined the common understanding of the word 'accident' to argue that under an insurance claim a cot-death might constitute an accident. An example of a linguist giving evidence of language use is discussed below. Roger Shuy, an eminent

American forensic linguist, argues that although John DeLorean, a sports car manufacturer, was set up to be involved in a nefarious drug deal, examination of the covert tapes show that he did not understand that this was the case and that because of this he never consented to take part (Shuy 1993).

identification evidence

Forensic linguists tend to agree that there is no such thing as a linguistic fingerprint; a consistent way in which an individual uses language across different situations and contexts. As discussed in the chapter on profiling and case linkage, however, it does seem that we fall into habits of repeating behaviours and in this tendency language behaviour is no different. In language individuals seem to reuse words, phrases and linguistic constructions, and this can be useful if the author of a text needs to be identified.

One of the highest profile cases where this tendency has been useful involved an FBI investigation into an individual who became known as the Unabomber. On 19 September 1995 *The Washington Post* published a 35,000 word supplement entitled 'The Industrial Society and its Future' which became known as the *Unabomber Manifesto*. The publication was a result of threats from 'the terrorist group FC' to continue and escalate a bombing campaign which had begun with a letter bomb in May 1978. The language of the manifesto was analysed by a variety of linguists (and others) at different stages in the investigation. For example, Roger Shuy (1993) analysed the text and provided the FBI with an indication of the sort of individuals who might have written the *Manifesto* in terms of their social and educational background. A further analysis by FBI agent Jim Fitzgerald attempted to identify what seemed to him to be unusual linguistic features and turns of phrase. Fitzgerald's analysis proved particularly useful when some comparison texts were brought forward. These texts were produced for the FBI when the sister-in-law of a Montana recluse, Ted Kaczynski, recognized in the manifesto his particular style of writing. In letters and other texts from Kaczynski some of the striking turns of phrase were repeated. A good example of one of these phrases is, 'You can't eat your cake and have it too.' This turning round of the more common formulation appeared both in the *Manifesto* and the known writings of Kaczynski. The linguistic evidence was reanalysed and defended in court by Don Foster, a Professor of English literature, and led to a search of Kaczynski's mountain cabin and the discovery of bomb-making equipment and other evidence leading to his conviction.

Technical acoustic analysis can also play a part in providing forensic identification evidence. On 9 September 2001, Major Charles Ingram of the British army became a contestant in the game show *Who Wants to be Millionaire?* The structure of the game is very straightforward: to win a million pounds the contestant simply has to answer 15 multiple choice questions in a row correctly. The Major, however, answered the questions in a curious way: when asked a question he talked through each of the four possible answers and whilst he was doing so a cough indicating the correct answer was heard from the audience. The Special Investigations Branch of New Scotland Yard approached forensic linguist and phonetician Peter French to see if he could identify the person producing the cough. Close analysis of the positions of the television studio microphone 'feeds' and the recorded decibel level (volume) of the coughs indicated the coughing had to come from the microphones directed at five of the ten candidate contestants known as 'fastest finger first' contestants. As one of the five contestants was a woman and the coughs definitely male, this left just four possible candidate coughers. One of the suspect coughs was different from the others; it seemed to be followed very closely by the muffled exclamation 'No!' possibly indicating to the Major that he was about to choose the wrong answer. Technical voice comparison indicated that the voice of the person saying 'No!' was consistent with instances of the word 'no' in the police interview of one of the candidates, Tecwen Whittock. This analysis was used in the trial of Charles and Diana Ingram (Ingram's wife) and Tecwen Whittock and all three were convicted of conspiracy.

Considering these two cases raises a major issue about linguistic identification evidence. In phonetic evidence there are, in fact, a few features of voices which are relatively constant within individuals or change in predictable ways. For example, the basic pitch of a person's voice, known as the formant frequency, is one such feature. Because variation in formant frequency (between different groups, such as men and women) is fairly well understood and can be described, this measure can be used straightforwardly in identification or exclusion questions. For example, a man with a high voice may be relatively unusual and so will be easier to identify than a man with a mid-range or deep voice. However, for most aspects used to describe voices and for nearly all of the factors concerning the choice of words or the grammatical construction of sentences, information like this on the distribution of features is not known and may be impossible to acquire. Language provides enormous possibility for variety and people use this variety creatively, both consciously and unconsciously. We use language differently with our lover, our colleagues and our boss; differently when we write or dictate, speak on the telephone or in face-to-face conversation; and we use language differently if we are happy, excited or depressed. Coping with this natural variation in individuals' language is one of the big challenges in forensic linguistic identification and it is an area in which much research is being carried out. What this research attempts to understand is how an individual's language is likely to behave across different situations; if this can be achieved, comparison and identification evidence will be able to move further down the road from a matter of opinion to a scientific discipline.

evidence of meaning and use

So far two sorts of linguistic evidence have been discussed, evidence of linguistic competence – Could the speaker understand or communicate sufficiently for the judicial process? – and evidence of identification – Did the person say this or write this? The final area in which linguists have tended to give evidence is over disputes of meaning and use. A good example of this is Roger Shuy's defence of John DeLorean the manufacturer of DeLorean cars. At the moment his business was about to go bust, DeLorean was subject to a sting operation by the US Drug Enforcement Agency (DEA). The DEA alleged that DeLorean had knowingly agreed to take money from the illegal drugs trade in order to finance his business. Shuy carried out a close linguistic analysis of the tapes between DeLorean and the DEA's undercover agent (actually a known con man acting to reduce the charges against him) and argued that DeLorean never agreed to the deal.

The basis of Shuy's work is a straightforward form of conversation analysis known as topic analysis. Even the more general findings from such an analysis can be revealing. For example, Shuy noted that in the passage he analysed, DeLorean introduces only a quarter of the topics whilst three-quarters of the agenda is set by the DEA agent. At the finer level Shuy shows how ambiguity in the conversation is used by the agents and how in particular one topic, 'interim financing', is understood by DeLorean to mean financing for his car business and understood by the agent and the prosecution to mean financing for the drug deal. Shuy argued that the prosecution were in a sense caught by their own sting. Because they understood the conversation to be about drug dealing they thought they had shown DeLorean discussing a drug deal. The close analysis reveals that from DeLorean's perspective the conversation was about financing for his car business. DeLorean was acquitted of the charges.

Shuy's and others work shows that close linguistic analysis can assist in trials such as DeLorean's. They show that it is not the case that presence at a conversation about drug dealing necessarily implies agreement to a deal. Linguistic analysis can reveal where presence at a discussion of illegal activity moves to agreement in participation in that activity and where it does not.

courtroom language

As well as sometimes participating in court cases, forensic linguists also have an academic interest in the workings of the courtroom. They have performed analyses of courtroom questioning by lawyers, of witness language and of judges' language in their rulings and in their instructions to juries. Through analysis of language, understanding can be gained of how power works in the courtroom, of how witnesses are likely to respond to certain types of questions and of what is likely to confuse or inform juries. One area which has been well examined is that of rape trials. The crime of rape is clearly a very serious one and whether someone is convicted can depend upon the question of consent. Consent, (i.e. whether the alleged rape victim agreed to have sex) is predominantly a question of communication and thus language use. A further issue often given prominence by feminist researchers is the way women victims of rape are treated by the legal system. It is argued that the process and in particular the opposing lawyers can create a very negative experience for the woman which can amount to re-victimization. It can further be argued that society's wider attitudes to sexual behaviour and relationships between the sexes can all be examined through the microcosm of a rape trial.

One example of a linguistic analysis of rape trials is Susan Ehrlich's (2001) work. She examines battles between the accused and the prosecuting lawyer as revealed in their grammatical usage. Thus Ehrlich shows how the lawyer's questions presuppose the defendant's responsibility for his actions: 'you proceeded to touch her', 'you laid down beside her' and 'you then started kissing her'. The defendant's response is to diffuse this and represent the actions back to the lawyer as joint actions; 'we started kissing', 'we started to fool around again' or actions of indeterminate nature 'all our clothes at one point were taken off and we were fooling around'. As well as giving insight into the tactics of legal examination, Ehrlich examines how the various participants in the trial have opposing conceptions of the nature of consent. When the defendant is asked how he knows that 'this wasn't something that she didn't want to do' he replies 'she never said "no", she never said "stop" and when I was kissing her she was kissing me back' (Ehrlich, 2003, p. 123). This construction of consent as being presumed, unless clearly withdrawn, links with Erhlich's ideological discussion of USA rape law. Until the 1950s this law required a woman to 'resist to the utmost' if unwanted intercourse was to be recognized as rape. It can be argued that although the law has been reformed, the courtroom exchanges reveal that the ideology it reflected still existed.

As well as exchanges between witness and lawyer, courtroom linguists are interested in the communication between judge and jury. One of the judges' tasks in UK and US trials is to explain the law to juries so that they can apply the evidence of the case to come to their verdict. However, these judicial instructions have multiple audiences: not only are judges talking to the jury and others present in the courtroom, their words will also be examined carefully to see if there are grounds for appeal to a higher court. Because of this, in some jurisdictions standard, legally watertight instructions have been published. Unfortunately, the concern to be legally watertight has led to some instructions being largely incomprehensible to the ordinary men and women of the jury. Linguists have recently argued for and been involved in attempts to reform these instructions to answer the needs of both audiences. In the UK Chris Heffer argues that jury instructions should be seen as a teaching exercise. Heffer suggests that best understanding by the jury would be achieved if instructions were given early in a trial and involve repetition and fully relevant examples of how the legal points might be applied to the case being considered. The model, he suggests, should be one of a teacher explaining something complex to a class. The current reality is very far removed from this. There are some examples, when a jury has asked for further explanation of an issue, where the judge has simply re-read the instruction to the jury. Faced with cases like this it may seem that a judge or the legal system is simply being obstinate but the judge has to be cautious; there is good research to demonstrate that how the law is explained to the jury can influence its verdict. For example, in many jurisdictions a jury should only convict a defendant if it believes that the case has been made against them 'beyond reasonable doubt'. This concept of 'reasonable doubt' has been explained to juries in different ways across different jurisdictions. Lawrence Solan charted some of these variations, ranging from 'actual and substantial doubt', and 'not a mere possible doubt', to 'not a conjecture or fanciful doubt' and 'abiding conviction of guilt'. Solan and other researchers show how these different constructions affect the jury's decision-making and can lead either to higher or lower conviction rates.

CALIFORNIA JUDICIAL CODE INSTRUCTIONS ON REASONABLE DOUBT

Previous instruction (CALJIC 2.90)

Reasonable doubt is defined as follows: It is not a mere possible doubt; because everything relating to human affairs is open to some possible or imaginary doubt. It is that state of the case which, after the entire comparison and consideration of all the evidence, leaves the minds of the jurors in that condition that they cannot say they feel an abiding conviction of the truth of the charge.

Reformed instruction (CALCRIM 220)

Proof beyond a reasonable doubt is proof that leaves you with an abiding conviction that the charge is true. The evidence need not eliminate all possible doubt because everything in life is open to some possible or imaginary doubt.

Taken from the website www.languageandlaw.org

One recent success in linguistic reform of the legal system has been Peter Tiersma's work with the Californian Judicial Council which in August 2005 agreed new plain language jury instructions. These instructions were the result of a committee to which Tiersma contributed. The reformed instruction on reasonable doubt is given above.

legal language reform

The reform of legal language is not restricted to courtroom situations. If you have ever signed any kind of contract whether for a credit card, a telephone or a property rental agreement you will have encountered legal language. If you have actually read such a contract you may have noticed that it is difficult to understand. In their search for reform, linguists have not only studied the nature of legal language but also tried to understand why legal language is as it is. In their efforts to understand and provide explanations for the difficulties of legal language, linguists have come up with two main answers. The first draws on the history of our legal systems; the second is more functional in trying to understand the purpose of legal language.

Peter Tiersma's (1999) book on legal language traces the history of the adversarial legal system from its origins in William the Conqueror's invasion of England in 1066. Before the Norman Conquest, written law appeared either in English or Latin but immediately following the Conquest all legal texts moved into Latin. Over a period of time Norman French became established in England as the language of the ruling class and gradually filtered through to the language of the law. As Tiersma observes, the first French statute does not appear in English law until 1275, more than 200 years after the Conquest. For the next 200 years or so, French became the dominant language of legal texts: the main exceptions to this was in the field of Church law. Henry VII's defeat of Richard III at the Battle of Bosworth in 1485 brought about abrupt and sweeping legal reforms. Henry was determined to establish his rather shaky claim to the English throne and introduced extensive legal reforms as part of the break with the past. These reforms saw the introduction of English as the language of statutes and parliamentary debates.

Evidence of this history can be found in modern legal language. Norman French influence can be found in vocabulary items such as *assault, misdemeanour, slander, tort* and so on but also in some grammatical structures. Perhaps the most obvious example is the French ordering of adjectives after the noun, thus giving us *court martial, attorney general* and *letters patent* rather than the more Anglicized *martial court, general attorney* and *patent letters.* Latin vocabulary and structures are also found. Good examples include *habeas corpus* (the right to be taken before a court after a certain period of arrest) and *mens rea* (referring to a person's culpable mental state with regard to a crime, e.g. intentionally harming someone or driving recklessly). The question as to why these historical structures and phrases remain in the language can be debated. One cynical explanation is that the legal profession has an interest in the language remaining specialized and inaccessible to the lay person. The counter argument to this is that the specialized words and use of words allows for the precision that is necessary in the legal context. One further argument for their maintenance is that the operation of the law requires stability of linguistic meanings. If a law is changed just to reform its language, it is very easy to slightly change its meaning or at least allow lawyers to argue for new interpretations on behalf of their clients.

These arguments in support of the historic use of legal language lead on to the second explanation as to why legal language can be so obscure and difficult to understand. The precision required in legal language requires it to be as context independent as possible. Most language depends on the wider context to be understood. The understanding of language is rarely dependent on the words alone. Not only do we use words like 'this' or 'that' which may require gestures to accompany them but also we make assumptions relating to social contexts. If I ask 'How are you?' I expect different responses if I ask the question at work or at a hospital bedside and the given response depends upon shared knowledge of what is socially appropriate. Legal language, especially the language of contracts, cannot be like this. It requires precision and understanding to be stable across situation and time. This has led both to a technical vocabulary and repetition of phrases where the meaning has been well established between lawyers. As everyday language moves on and meanings subtly move and change, the technical vocabulary remains static and becomes more and more difficult for the lay person to understand. John Gibbons (2003) provides an example of an Anglo-Saxon will of Wulfwyn showing, amongst other things, how context-dependent it is. Thus Wulfwyn leaves some of his possessions to 'my lady' and 'my royal lord' without actually naming these individuals and even includes the phrase 'Stanhard is to have everything I have bequeathed to him' (Gibbons, 2003, p. 27). In contrast the formulaic modern will requires names and addresses and a specificity not found in the earlier version. In spite of its apparent precise use of language, the modern will still contains curious features and redundancies which relate to the historic language. Gibbons (2003) and Tiersma (1999) both point out that every will is a 'last will' and Gibbons points out that his own will contains the phrase 'I give, devise and bequeath' (p. 26). Items such as these are clearly open to reform.

conclusions

Forensic linguistics then is a field of research and practice which covers much ground. The legal and judicial systems depend upon language, and experts in language can usefully apply their methods and insights to assist, criticize and attempt reforms. In addition to this we have seen some of the areas in which language experts can provide evidence to the courts. Some of the topics of interest to forensic linguists overlap with or have parallels with forensic psychology. Psychologists, for example, may be interested in individuals who are excluded from full participation in the legal system because they are in some way psychologically vulnerable. Linguists, for their part, can become involved in cases where an individual may be linguistically vulnerable. Psychologists too are interested in courtroom processes and relationships and can study courtroom language in pursuing these interests, and in this field there is certainly room for psychologists and linguists to collaborate. Some psychologists, for example, are interested in the processes of legal decision-making but appear to pay little attention to how decision-making processes may have changed over the history of the law in civil society. Different types of decision-making might be identified through historic studies of the changing legal frameworks and this could lead to greater understanding of what occurs today and how it might be improved. On the other hand there is very little linguistic work on offenders. A few studies have examined sex offenders' narratives of their offences and there are general studies of prisoner language but these have yet to find applications. As both disciplines move forward there is likely to be a degree of convergence in some of these areas, but the distinctions and differing interests can provide richness and perspective in a shared field of study.

recommended further reading

Cotterill, J. (2003) *Language and power in court: A linguistic analysis of the O. J. Simpson trial.* Basingstoke: Palgrave Macmillan.

Ehrlich, S. (2001) *Representing rape: Language and sexual consent.* New York: Routledge.

Foster, D. (2001) *Author unknown: On the trail of anonymous*, 2nd edn. London: Macmillan.

Gibbons, J. (2003) *Forensic linguistics: An introduction to language in the justice system.* Melbourne, Australia: Blackwell Publishers.

McMenamin, G. R. (2002) *Forensic linguistics – advances in forensic stylistics.* Boca Raton, FL: CRC Press.

Shuy, R. (1993) *Language crimes: The use and abuse of language evidence in the courtroom.* Oxford: Blackwell Publishers.

Tiersma, P. M. (1999) *Legal language.* Chicago, IL: University of Chicago Press.

For more academic interest the journal of the International Association of Forensic Linguists, *Speech Language and the Law (University of Birmingham Press)*, contains papers and research articles which cover the full scope of forensic linguistic research.

punishment and offenders

Punishment involves some form of pain, discomfort, or generally unpleasant experience. It can take many forms, such as psychological, financial, emotional or physical suffering. It is for this reason that the punishment of crime becomes such a moral dilemma: bringing about debate as to who should have the right to punish others, who decides what is punishable and what is not, and what form punishment should take. What is considered acceptable by society, to what extent this differs between societies or cultures, and how has this changed throughout history will be just some of the topics discussed in this chapter.

history and philosophy of punishment

The nature of punishment for wrongdoing, just as the nature of crime, changes over time and across cultures. Actions or behaviour which are now acceptable within most Western cultures – for example homosexuality and abortion – were not in the past. Just as crimes have changed, so too have punishments. Now, most people would wince at the thought of punishing someone for blasphemy by tying them to a piece of fencing and dragging them through the streets of the local town, but they may still find the death penalty acceptable, or would think that a community-based penalty for non-payment of a fine is an appropriate punishment. While punishments may change, they are still based on a small number of theories for punishing offenders.

In Anglo-Saxon England, the aim of punishment for crime was to stop physical retaliation by victims' families. So, if someone killed a man, the murderer had to pay 100 shillings to the victim's family. It seems that some sort of monetary compensation for loss was preferable to a physical punishment, and only repeat offenders were punished by having part of their body removed or injured in some manner.

In the sixteenth century a London writer, Robert Greene, noted that crime was becoming like entertainment and this meant that more and more often reports of offences and their punishments were appearing in newspapers, journals and chronicles. There were reports of poisoners being boiled in cauldrons, thieves being whipped, rapists being branded, prostitutes being tied to posts with notes declaring their offences pinned to their dresses, debtors being tied backwards to horses and taken around a town, and bigamists being drawn (dragged from place to place on a piece of wood behind a horse) and then burned. The public shaming of offenders played a big part of punishments until the middle of the sixteenth century, but public hangings carried on for a long time after this in the UK and parts of Europe (think about the guillotining of the aristocracy in Revolutionary France), which might also be seen as shameful for the offenders and their families.

Much of the punishment described above is based on retribution. Retribution can take many forms – paying a victim's family or being shamed for the things that you have done. Shame or guilt and their part in punishment is a key element in Judaism, Christianity and Islam, and there is a clear cross-over within Christian-based cultures between what is 'sinful' and what is illegal. If someone has committed a crime, then he or she has to be punished for what he or she has done; for what has gone on in the past. Criminals have to 'pay' for what they have done, they 'owe a debt' to society or a victim. This is the notion of 'just deserts', that offenders are subject to a punishment that is equal to the crime that they have committed. So, a mugger is not likely to be executed, and a murderer is not likely be sentenced to a community penalty. Retributive punishments do enable sentencers to come up with a tariff of punishments which should be implemented equally. All offenders who have committed a drink-driving offence will be given the same sentence; all offenders who have raped another person will be given a similar punishment. However, such retributive punishment demands that someone is to 'blame' for a criminal offence and considers that all offenders are equal. Think about whether a woman who has been subjected to twenty years of domestic abuse and kills her husband during an incident is to 'blame' in the same way as a woman who kills her husband because she wishes to leave him and be with her lover. Consider whether there is a difference between a shoplifter who steals to feed a drug habit to one who steals to feed his or her children. Retribution is not concerned with whether an offender will change in the future; it is about what someone has done.

Sentencers did not start to think about punishment as a deterrent for offenders until the mid-1800s. Deterring offenders from taking part in crimes, discouraging others from taking part in illegal activities, or putting criminals somewhere that they could not offend again, which will all reduce crime rates, are the key element of reductivism. However, reductivism is often linked to severe penalties for crimes – long prison sentences or capital punishment, which makes this form of punishment a little controversial in some people's minds. If a twenty-year prison sentence will stop a criminal from stealing again, then so be it. If executing a murderer will make another person stop and think twice about carrying out a crime, then reductivism has been successful. However, this form of punishment relies on a rational thinking-offender for effect. It assumes that an offender will weigh up the pros and cons of committing a crime, decide that the punishment is not worth the gain from the crime and decide not to steal, vandalize, or kill. This form of reasoning, known as Utilitarianism, was developed by the English philosopher Jeremy Bentham during the early 1800s.

During the early 1990s in the UK, much of sentencing policy was based on this concept of deterrence, rather than the rehabilitation of offenders which became popular during the 1950s and 1960s. However, during the later 1990s another element of punishment came to the fore, that of reform or rehabilitation. This is based on getting offenders to consider their past behaviour and think about changing their future behaviour – going from being criminals to law-abiding citizens.

Anglo-American sentencers tend to be eclectic in their development and implementation of punishments. The range of punishments available, and acceptable, are a mixture of the retributive and reductivist.

attitudes and beliefs in punishment

We are used to the notion of society or the State punishing lawbreakers for their wrongdoings, but what do *citizens* actually think about punishment, and *who* should be punished? This section explores people's attitudes towards punishment, what happens when the State does not punish wrongdoers and whether it is right for communities to take the law into their own hands and punish deviants.

There has been a great deal of research conducted by criminologists, sociologists and psychologists exploring attitudes towards punishment, various forms of punishment and sentencing beliefs. Many have found differences between groups, for example based on gender, age, socio-economic status, race, political and religious beliefs. Despite the large volume of research, there are few current theories that attempt to incorporate the findings into one unified theory.

An American criminologist, Franklin Zimring (2003), has attempted to draw together historical data, exploring patterns in these data with current research to help him inform theory. He suggests that there are two models of punishment values which he refers to as: 'due process' and 'vigilante tradition' beliefs. Most people share the beliefs of one of these two categories. Those who believe in due process values believe that offenders are difficult to identify, and this makes policing and punishment difficult. Partly due to concern about not identifying the correct perpetrator and accusing the wrong person of a crime, due process supporters advocate that it is better that ten guilty people go free than one innocent person be punished.

The vigilante tradition model suggests that law, order and policing are the responsibility of the community, partly because of a distrust of the State. Offenders are easily identifiable within the community and are enemies of the community rather than being the community's own members. Mistakes are not made. Due to this confidence in punishing the correct person, the use of force is encouraged in achieving the communities' goals. By punishing criminals it allows greater freedom and safety within the community for law-abiding citizens.

Zimring uses historical data to explore the links between vigilante values in America, with its history of lynching. Using data which goes back as far as 1882 he found that the southern states had the highest recorded history of lynching. More recent data also shows that the southern states have the highest rates of justifiable homicides, and the most frequent use of the death penalty. He suggests that this is due to the strong tradition of vigilante values and beliefs held by many US citizens, especially in the southern states.

Advocates of the vigilante tradition often favour the use of the death penalty because of their confidence in their justice system and the belief that mistakes are not made, while advocates of the due process model fear the use of the death penalty because it is an irreversible punishment. While Britain no long allows the death penalty as a punishment for crime, people's lives can still be ruined if they are wrongfully imprisoned. There have been many highly publicized cases of miscarriages of justice in Britain in the last couple of decades, such as the Birmingham Six, the Guildford Four and the Cardiff Three. Recent cases regarding shaken baby syndrome also bring into question the authority of expert witnesses in court, and the reliability of the criminal justice process. Given the history of miscarriages of justice known to the British public and the dramatic media attention they have received, it is not surprising that most British citizens follow the due process model.

While highly publicized miscarriages of justice concerning those who have been wrongfully imprisoned are of great concern to the public, so too are those cases whereby offenders have not been punished for the crimes they have committed. This is especially difficult when the offender is known to the police, or in some cases the victim or the victim's family. It is conditions such as these that make vigilantism most likely.

vigilantism

Vigilantism is a situation in which a citizen or group of citizens take the law into their own hands. The most common cause for this action is when citizens believe that they cannot get justice through legal means, i.e. through the criminal justice system. Despite the terms 'vigilante' and 'vigilantism' being used frequently in the media, little attention has been drawn to this issue within academia, even in terms of understanding what this phenomenon actually is. British criminologist, Professor Les Johnston (1996) attempted to provide a definition of vigilantism as a starting point for further investigation. In conceptualizing this phenomenon he suggests that there are six components to vigilante behaviour.

First, he suggests that vigilantism involves some degree of planning and premeditation. This may only be minimal but it is important to distinguish between vigilante behaviour and self-defence. Second, vigilantism is a private and voluntary act. Therefore, it must be carried out by private citizens, not law enforcement agents. However, there are clearly some difficulties here, for example an off-duty police officer who participates in an activity that would normally constitute vigilantism. Third, the activity must have no support or authority from the state and is therefore autonomous. Fourth, it uses threats or force. Fifth, it is a reaction to crime or perceived social deviance (i.e. a crime may not even have been committed, but it is perceived to have taken place). And finally, it contributes to a personal or collective sense of security.

Vigilantes or vigilante groups may be organized in a variety of ways. Mark Button (2002) outlined different types of vigilantism based on the level of organization: the lone vigilante, the semi-organized group and the organized group.

The *lone vigilante* is best described by the case of Tony Martin who was repeatedly victimized by a group of youths in his remote farmhouse in the countryside. On several occasions youths had broken into his home and despite many calls to the police, Martin did not feel he was being taken seriously. In order to defend himself, he placed booby-traps around the premises, and kept a gun near his bed. One night two youths broke into the farmhouse and Martin fired several shots in the dark, resulting in the death of one intruder and injuring the second.

Semi-organized groups, as the term implies, are groups of citizens who gather together with little organizational structure. One of the most recent examples of a well-known publicized case in Britain took place in Paulsgrove estate, Portsmouth. In the summer of 2000, an eight-year-old schoolgirl, Sarah Payne, was murdered (elsewhere in the country) by a registered sex offender. Sarah's parents began campaigning for the sex offender register to be available to the public so that the community would know if there were paedophiles living in the vicinity. The *News of the World* newspaper then began a campaign of naming and shaming convicted paedophiles. Paulsgrove witnessed riots as local people took to the streets in order to protest about the paedophiles living in their community. These riots ended in violence with at least five innocent families being forced to flee from their homes and two individuals committing suicide. It was also alleged that several names, faces and addresses were incorrect, and so innocent people were being labelled as paedophiles and then hunted down by angry mobs.

There are many examples of *organized* vigilante groups throughout the world, some more acceptable than others, ranging from the Guardian Angels in New York, set up to protect New Yorkers on subways during the 1980s (when crime was rife and police were perceived to be inadequate), to the Triads of Hong Kong and paramilitaries in Northern Ireland. As can be seen from the examples, groups differ dramatically in their purpose, rationale and methods, all having different focus and consequences.

Vigilantism may take on a more policing-type function, or the form of distributing what is perceived to be an appropriate punishment for the (perceived) crime committed. The punishment may take the form of intimidation and threats, as well as physical suffering. It is a term which often conjures up images of lynch mobs. In the USA a content analysis of newspaper clippings of accounts of 60 lynchings committed between 1899 and 1946 found that the more people in the mob the greater the savagery and viciousness with which they killed their victims.

Thankfully today lynch mobs are very rare, but this does not mean that such activities do not take place. There are modern day examples throughout the world, such as in India, in August 2004, where over 200 women gathered together to claim justice for rape victims. Below are excerpts taken from the *Guardian* newspaper's report of the event concerning a man who was hacked to death in the courthouse by women he had (allegedly) raped.

> At 3pm on August 13 2004, Akku Yadav was lynched by a mob of around 200 women from Kasturba Nagar. It took them 15 minutes to hack to death the man they say raped them with impunity for more than a decade. Chilli powder was thrown in his face and stones hurled. As he flailed and fought, one of his alleged victims hacked off his penis with a vegetable knife. A further 70 stab wounds were left on his body. The incident was made all the more extraordinary by its setting. Yadav was murdered not in the dark alleys of the slum, but on the shiny white marble floor of Nagpur district court. Laughed at and abused by the police when they reported being raped by Yadav, the women took the law into their own hands. A local thug, Yadav and his gang had terrorized the 300 families of Kasturba Nagar for more than a decade, barging into homes demanding money, shouting threats and abuse. Residents say he murdered at least three neighbours and dumped their bodies on railway tracks. They had reported his crimes to the police dozens of times. Each time he was arrested, he was granted bail. But it was rape that Yadav used to break and humiliate the community. A rape victim lives in every other house in the slum, say the residents of Kasturba Nagar. He violated

women to control men, ordering his henchmen to drag even girls as young as 12 to a nearby derelict building to be gang-raped. In India, even to admit to being raped is taboo, yet dozens of Yadav's victims reported the crime. But the 32-year-old was never charged with rape. Instead, the women say, the police would tell him who had made the reports and he would come after them. According to residents, the police were hand-in-glove with Yadav: he fed the local officers bribes and drink, and they protected him. But his death has not brought the women peace. Five were immediately arrested, then released following a demonstration across the city. Now every woman living in the slum has claimed responsibility for the murder. They say no one person can take the blame: they have told the police to arrest them all. But it is Narayane who is in limbo as she waits for her case to be heard. 'After the murder, society's eyes opened: the police's failings came to light. That has irritated them. The police see me as a catalyst for the exposure and want to nip it in the bud.'

(*Guardian* 16 September 2005)

It is interesting to explore the way in which different countries perceive vigilante behaviour, or even what constitutes vigilantism. In Britain, for example, when Tony Martin shot and killed a burglar and injured the second, he was charged with murder (later reduced to manslaughter) and imprisoned. While there has been debate in Britain as to whether this was a 'just' punishment, he has spent many years in prison. In the United States many people keep guns in their home for self-defence and protection from intruders – this would be illegal in Britain. This brings into question how the rights of the citizen and the rights of an intruder should be balanced. Should citizens have the right to protect themself and potentially kill an intruder?

One of the many problems with vigilante groups is that the accused are unlikely to be given a fair trial or chance to legally defend themselves. The punishment is delivered without arrest, detention, trial or appeal. There are examples of cases throughout history where people have or could be accused of almost anything (e.g. witchcraft): in fact, whatever is socially undesirable at the time could be a target of vigilantism. It is this punishment aspect of vigilantism that often hits the headlines, and which is the most common feature of vigilantism in most people's conception. However intimidation or the threat of violence can also have a severe effect upon the accused.

One aspect of criminal victimization that is often overlooked is the amount of emotion involved. Being a victim of crime, or having a friend or family member who has been criminally victimized can provoke a huge amount of emotion about the wrongs committed against them, prompting some to take justice in any way they can. However, it may be questioned whether vigilantes gain justice or revenge. And does it matter?

cross-cultural punishment

As noted above, punishment often reflects the prevailing culture, norms and attitudes in a society. For example, punishing the body in order to punish the spirit was originally the basis of corporal punishments, but within Western cultures this moved towards punishment of the mind through imprisonment (Foucault, 1991).

Imprisonment as a form of punishment is found in many cultures. There are a number of different ideas behind why imprisonment may be a good punishment. It can be argued that depriving offenders of freedom illustrates that by breaking society's rules then you are removed from that society and are not able to take part and do the things that citizens take for granted. Imprisonment also means that the offender is unable to offend against the rest of society, known as 'incapacitation', though the offender may continue to offend in some way while in prison (e.g. assaulting other prisoners, drug taking etc.).

One topic that is often debated is whether the removal of freedom is enough of a punishment or whether the conditions in prison should also be as harsh as possible. The idea behind this is that if prison is made into a really horrible place to be, then offenders will not want to go back and so will not reoffend. However, it may well be that offenders just learn how to commit future crimes to minimize the chances of being caught. It is also often felt that offenders should be made to suffer while imprisoned and should not have luxuries. This suggests that the removal of freedom is not enough, particularly for crimes against children, sexual crimes or murder, and certainly that prison should not be seen as an alternative home setting.

In some countries the notion of keeping people in prison is taken one step further with the execution of offenders. Again, this is thought to serve a number of purposes. It not only means that offenders are no longer able to offend, it may also deter other people from offending in that way if they know they could be executed, and in some countries (e.g. the USA) it is seen as an element of closure for the victim's families and follows the 'eye for an eye' idea of retributive justice.

The number of countries which have capital punishment is decreasing. The USA is alone in Western countries in retaining the death penalty. Countries within the European Union are generally bound by the European Convention on Human Rights which stipulates that the death penalty is not an appropriate punishment. Other countries which do have the death penalty include Singapore, Japan, China, Saudi Arabia and Iran. Of all the countries retaining the death penalty, the majority of executions in 2004 were carried out, in order of number of executions, in China, Iran, Vietnam, USA and Saudi Arabia (Amnesty International, 2005).

The types of crime which carry a death penalty differ. In the USA the death penalty is reserved for murder, in other countries it can be given for homosexuality, drug dealing or smuggling.

Methods of execution also differ. In the USA there have been moves to make executions as humane as possible. This has led to the change from hanging to the electric chair, to gas and finally lethal injection (though the humaneness of the lethally injected drugs is currently being questioned). The idea behind this appears to be that if the State is going to kill someone it should be done without torture and cruelty.

In other countries very different methods are used. In some countries beheading is considered a way of carrying out a death sentence because decapitation is felt in some cultures to be a method of execution which shows the skill of the executioner – this used to be

ISLAMIC PUNISHMENTS

There are four different types of punishment in Islam (Saney, 2005):

- *Hodoud* are specific punishments in the *Qur'an* or mentioned by the Prophet, and include cutting off the hands of thieves and lashes for the drinking of alcohol.
- *Ghesas* are those punishments borrowed from other cultures.
- *Diyeh* is the system of fines and money where victims/relatives may accept money from the offender.
- The fourth type are those milder punishments e.g. less than eighty lashes.

the method of execution for the nobility in England. It has also been suggested to be quick and painless (this was the reason given for the development in France of the guillotine), but doubts about this led to decapitation being eliminated in many countries as stories emerged of moving eyes and lips on decapitated heads.

In Islamic cultures notions of punishment can be different from those in other cultures. The Islamic system seems to focus more on compensating the victims than punishing the offenders but is also about not alienating the offenders so that they are not lost to the community. Therefore, imprisonment is not generally used.

Islamic punishments are more personal because they are about a relationship between the offender and the victim. A number of Western cultures have started moving towards this notion of a relationship between the victim, the offender and the wider community, and compensation is seen in the Restorative Justice movement (discussed further below).

One method of execution often discussed in relation to Islamic Law is that of stoning, which is not used in many countries because it is often felt to be inhumane and painful for the offender. However, some advocates of the death penalty believe that pain-free capital punishment is no punishment at all and there have been calls within the USA to stop making executions painless.

modern punishment

In an attempt to tackle current concerns about crime, a number of Western countries are changing how they deal with offenders. It has been argued that Western countries have become much more punitive, giving harsher penalties than thirty years ago. Part of this is a belief that the liberalist policies of the 1960s and early 1970s were not effective and that there is currently a crime epidemic, particularly with drug-related and anti-social crime. There is a tension between the belief that offenders can be in some sense 'treated' in order to prevent offending behaviour (for example, through the use of cognitive behavioural therapies) and the belief that offenders need to be punished and that the punishment alone should be enough to teach people. If the punishment does not do this, it is not harsh enough. This has led to a number of schools of thought about punishments.

The first is that punishment should also be about helping offenders to change the way they think about their crimes, about their victims and about offending in general. One method of doing this is through offender treatment programmes which are discussed in more detail elsewhere in this book.

However, some people think that this concentrates too much on the needs of the offender and not on the needs of the victim and of society. One method of trying to adjust this balance is by the use of Restorative Justice. It has been argued that current punishment does not require offenders to acknowledge (i) the consequences of their anti-social actions and (ii) their indifference to the needs of crime victims. This approach believes that victims are alienated from the criminal justice process because crime is defined as wrong-doing against the laws of the State. This is why, in Western societies, the State is generally responsible for prosecuting cases and not the victim. Supporters of restorative justice believe that the offender owes a debt to the victim, not just the State. This may involve mediation between the offender and the victim (or wider community), community work, written apologies or the payment of money to the victim. The notion of reconciliation is important as it is thought that the main way this works to reduce reoffending is to make offenders recognize that they have done wrong: if the offender is given the opportunity to show regret and be re-accepted into the community, this will benefit all (Easton and Piper, 2005).

However, some people believe that the current criminal justice process is too soft on offenders – there are often calls for prison sentences to be longer and harsher. This has led to developments such as chain gangs where physical labour is seen as an important part of the punishment. Newman (1983) argued that offenders should be given corporal punishment rather than prison, unless they were repeat offenders or their crime reached a certain threshold. Therefore, prison would only be for the worst kind of offenders. He argued that electric shock should be the preferred method of punishment and believed that the community should be responsible for the punishments, which should take place in public, and that the offender would be 'redeemed' rather than 'rehabilitated'. This would also reduce the cost of prisons (because they were not being used so much) and give the community retribution by making offenders suffer physically for their crime. One of the bases of this view is that people choose to offend. This approach does not consider any of the criminological theories of offending behaviour (e.g. poverty, social structures, social influences and class). Newman (1983) believed that 'Punishment must, above all else be painful' (p. 6) and that 'pain ... is a necessary condition of justice' (p. 7). This is an interesting approach, particularly in response to the death penalty in the USA which some victims' families think is over-humane as the offender does not suffer in the way that the victim did.

Shaming is also something that is currently considered as a possible way of making offenders (particularly young offenders) think about their actions and prevent them from offending in future, as well as deterring others. In the UK in 2005, a suggestion was made by a member of the British parliament that offenders on community service punishment should be made to wear distinctive orange uniforms. There was a general feeling within the public that community service was a soft option: the reasoning behind this suggestion was that it would enable the public to see what those on community service actually had to do. There was, however, an outcry amongst some members of the community who felt this was much more about humiliation and making offenders stand out within the community in a negative way.

conclusions

One of the interesting aspects about punishment is its use regarding crime changes across time and cultures. Punishments that were well thought of twenty years ago may now be considered obsolete. It is likely that some of the current trends in punishment will also be rejected in a few years time. Punishment is a constantly evolving aspect of society and is linked to thoughts about safety, the effectiveness of the criminal justice system and emotional responses to victimization. Consider your own responses to crime and punishment. Do you think being a victim of crime alters your perceptions as to how offenders should be punished? Do you think punishment should include rehabilitation or should it be solely about making the offender suffer? These are questions which all those involved with punishment have to consider and are issues being researched by criminal psychologists.

further reading

Amnesty International (2005) *Facts and figures on the death penalty.* Accessed 19 September 2005 at http://web.amnesty.org/pages/deathpenalty-facts-eng.

Barrett, A. and Harrison, C. (eds) (1999) *Crime and punishment in England: A sourcebook.* London: UCL Press.

Button, M. (2002) *Private policing.* Cullompton, UK: Willan.

Cavadino, M. and Dignan, J. (1997) *The penal system: An introduction.* London: Sage.

Duff, R. A. (2001) *Punishment, communication and community.* Oxford: Oxford University Press.

Easton, S. and Piper, C. (2005) *Sentencing and punishment: The quest for justice.* Oxford: Oxford University Press.

Foucault, M. (1991) *Discipline and punish: The birth of the prison*, trans. A. Sheridan. London: Penguin Books Ltd.

Guardian, The (2004) *Arrest us all*. Accessed 3 October 2005 at http://www.guardian.co.uk/women/story/0,3604,1571406,00.html.

Johnston, L. (1996) What is vigilantism? *British Journal of Criminology, 36*, 220–36.

McLaughlin, E., Fergusson, R., Hughes, G. and Westmarland, L. (eds) (2003) *Restorative justice: Critical issues*. London: Sage.

Newman, G. (1983) *Just and painful: A case for the corporal punishment of criminals*. London: Macmillan.

Saney, P. (2005) Cultural dimensions of crime: The Islamic system of criminal justice. Paper presented at the XIV World Congress of Criminology, Philadelphia, USA.

Walker, N. (1991) *Why punish? Theories of punishment reassessed*. Oxford: Oxford University Press.

Zimring, F. (2003) The *contradictions of American capital punishment*. Oxford: Oxford University Press.

experiencing imprisonment

As we saw in chapter 1, many criminal psychologists work within prisons where they will assess, manage and treat offenders in their care with the aim of reducing their likelihood of reoffending on release from prison. In addition to these responsibilities, prison psychologists also conduct research related to imprisonment. Such research can aim to increase our understanding of what imprisonment is like with a view to enhancing rehabilitative efforts or it may focus on the evaluation of the effectiveness of psychological interventions in place. Academic criminal psychologists working in universities have also been conducting such research.

While chapter 10 outlines the research on the rehabilitation of offenders, this chapter will introduce you to the research conducted on how being imprisoned can affect prisoners and how they cope with this experience.

So, when considering the numbers of people affected by imprisonment, how many are we actually talking about? According to the International Centre for Prison Studies there are over 8.5 million people imprisoned worldwide. Although this is a very high number, should we really be concerned about how imprisonment affects these people? Some newspaper reports would suggest not. I am sure you have seen newspaper reports stating that prison is 'too easy' and is more like a 'holiday camp' than a prison. In contrast, there have been numerous documentaries and television series which have shown a more unpleasant and distressing side to imprisonment. Unless we have visited a prison or have been imprisoned ourselves, most of what we know of imprisonment comes from the television or other media. But with these conflicting reports of what prison is like it is difficult to know whether we should be concerned about the 8.5 million people currently imprisoned.

Psychologists and other social scientists have been researching the effects of imprisonment for some time. Much of this research has been conducted in the West: its findings might not apply so readily to prisons in other parts of the world and it is important to bear this in mind. The research that has been conducted has found that imprisonment can have very negative effects for some prisoners. This can result from the actual experience of being imprisoned or it can be related to a person's encounters with others whilst imprisoned.

characteristics of the prison environment

When some newspaper reports condemn prisons for being more like holiday camps and state that life in prison is too easy, they are contrasting what they believe prison to be like with the perceived goals of imprisonment. Specifically, they are focusing on the goals of punishment and deterrence. For prison to be a punishment it must be an uncomfortable experience. Another goal of imprisonment is deterrence. We often hear about the supposed deterrent effect of imprisonment when we hear politicians talking about 'getting tough on crime'. If the threat of imprisonment is to deter prisoners from reoffending or to deter otherwise law-abiding citizens from committing crime, imprisonment must be an unpleasant experience. But how unpleasant should it be? Some theorists have expressed their concerns that if the discomfort of imprisonment is too great, it can be counterproductive.

the physical environment

The prison environment is stressful by its very nature and several researchers have examined the stressors operating in prisons. Just being imprisoned results in a loss of freedom and a loss of autonomy. Your daily routine is dictated by the prison routine, and choices, such as what you will have for your dinner or what time you will get up in the morning, are no longer available. Because male and female prisoners are held separately, imprisonment also results in the loss of heterosexual relationships. Depending on the volume of prisoners being held in one institution, prisons can also be very noisy and overcrowded. Sharing a cell with another prisoner means you have little privacy, as can the physical design of the prison. In some prisons, the front of a cell is composed of open bars which denies the prisoner any privacy at all. Depending on the resources in the prison and the prison routine, inmates might spend a great deal of time in their cells and some can find this enforced inactivity stressful. It is therefore quite easy to understand why the prison environment itself can result in prisoners experiencing stress.

At this point, it is important to make a distinction between sentenced and remand prisoners, and consider how their status can affect their experience of imprisonment. Remand prisoners have yet to be convicted of the crime they are alleged to have committed and therefore they have the additional concerns of their forthcoming trial and legal representation. In the UK remand and sentenced prisoners are held in the same institutions, whereas in the US prisoners who are waiting for their case to be tried are located not in prisons but in jails. In comparison to prisons in the US, jails are notoriously poorly resourced, with inactivity and crowding being particular problems.

the social environment

As well as these stressors of the physical prison environment, there are additional stressors that prisoners must endure; those associated with the *experience* of imprisonment and the social environment. Some of these relate to the outside world whereas others relate to the internal world of the prison.

In relation to stressors in the outside world, prisoners can be concerned about the loss of their employment and their relationships with their families, and how these will be affected by their imprisonment. This would particularly be the case for prisoners with longer sentences.

The enforced removal of prisoners from their social network and from intimate relationships with others can result in loneliness. Loneliness can be separated into two types: emotional loneliness is experienced when you do not have a close, intimate attachment with another person. Prisoners who are separated from partners might experience such loneliness. Social loneliness, on the other hand, is where you are not part of an engaging social network. On being imprisoned, you no longer have access to your friends and work colleagues and may find yourself in the company of strangers. It is quite likely that partners and families of prisoners will also experience both emotional and social loneliness. However, not all prisoners will experience loneliness on imprisonment. For example, prisoners who are part of an established criminal network may find it easier to integrate into the prison social network if they have co-offenders imprisoned with them at the same time. Also some prisoners might experience one type of loneliness but not the other.

With regard to stressors within the prison, the social environment of prisons can be a source of stress. A subculture of violence exists within some prisons, with physical violence being approved by some prisoners. For some prisoners prison might therefore be a very different environment from what they were used to in the outside world and therefore being imprisoned can require a lot of adjustment. The social environment among prisoners can be viewed as a hierarchy. Because violence and being able to protect yourself is valued within prison, violent prisoners may have the greatest status and sit at the top of the hierarchy. Being imprisoned can therefore quite reasonably result in fears about experiencing violence at the hands of other inmates. Prisoners might also feel they have to change the way they would normally behave in the outside world to ensure they do not end up at the bottom of the hierarchy.

Bullying amongst prisoners or victimization, as other researchers refer to it, has been well researched by criminal psychologists and other social scientists such as Jane Ireland and Kimmett Edgar. The types of bullying behaviours that occur in prison include direct and indirect forms of victimization. Direct forms are those where the aggressors inflict the aggressive act directly on the victims, for example, by hitting them, whereas indirect victimization is where the aggression is delivered in such a way that the aggressors cannot be associated with it. It could include encouraging others to exclude the victims from some activity. In addition, bullying behaviours can be physical or verbal, and hence targeted at the victim, or the victim's property might be the target.

The research literature has suggested that the types of bullying behaviour displayed varies depending on the bully's age, with direct forms of bullying being associated with younger offenders. In relation to gender, some research studies have found that male prisoners more often use direct forms of bullying than females do, whereas other studies have found no evidence of this.

The types of bullying behaviours experienced also seem to vary with culture. In prisons in the US, prisoners more frequently report sexual violence in comparison to their counterparts in UK prisons. It has been suggested that these differences could be due to the higher incidence of lethal violence in US society, racial tension within US prisons and staff's supportive attitudes to prison rape.

Bullying others and the experience of being bullied seems quite prevalent in prisons. Drawing comparisons between studies can, however, be problematic since the definitions used by different researchers have varied. It is therefore important to bear this in mind when considering the research that has been conducted. Using a timescale of the previous week, UK researchers found that forty-five per cent of their male adult and young offenders reported behaving in ways that were considered indicative of bullying others and forty per cent of prisoners reported experiencing such behaviours. Very similar percentages were found by Susie Grennan and Jessica Woodhams with their sample of young offenders. Using a different definition and a different approach, researchers in the US found that, on average, their male inmates were victimized once a month. From just these few statistics, it seems that being imprisoned brings with it a substantial risk of being victimized.

This raises the question of whether all prisoners are at equal risk of victimization. Some studies have found that both prison staff and prisoners reported that the prisoners who are more at risk were those that broke the inmate code. This code forbids the reporting of other prisoners to prison staff. Other studies have found that prisoners perceived as weaker, less experienced or socially isolated were more often targeted, as were those serving a sentence for a controversial crime, such as child sexual abuse. It also seems possible that the risk of being victimized varies depending on the security rating of the prison. For example, Jessica Woodhams found only two per cent of prisoners in a low security prison reported being bullied in the previous month.

Since prisoner bullying has been associated with failed rehabilitation and recidivism, self-injury by prisoners and poor psychological health, a good understanding of why it occurs is needed if criminal psychologists are going to help reduce bullying in prison. One possibility that researchers have suggested is that prisoners protect themselves from future victimization by victimizing others. This would seem to relate to the prisoner hierarchy, which, as noted above, reserves greater status for prisoners who act violently. Through bullying others, prisoners can obtain, from other inmates, resources that are of limited availability in prison, such as tobacco and telephone cards. If the bullies do not use these resources themselves, they can sell them on at a higher price. It has also been suggested that bullying might offer relief from tension and boredom. This proposal is supported by research from the US that found involvement in formal activities, such as educational and vocational programmes, to be associated with less prisoner violence. An alternative explanation for this finding could be that increased supervision during such activities prevents prisoner violence.

As noted above, prisoner victimization has been associated with a number of negative outcomes for prisoners. However, in what other ways can victimization impact on prisoners? If a motivation for bullying is for the bully to gain limited resources from the victim, it follows that one outcome for victims will be economic deprivation. This might also be the case if a victim's property is damaged. Physical injury is also likely with the more direct and physical forms of aggression. Social loneliness may result from rumour-spreading or ostracism if the peer group withdraws from the victim. These negative effects of being victimized in prison can be compounded by the inmate code, which discourages informing on fellow prisoners: it can be particularly difficult for prisoners to seek help from staff.

Clearly not all of these stressors will be present in every prison. Also, it is important to note that prisoners are individuals and their resilience to each stressor will vary. Whilst some may find the loss of autonomy unbearable, others will find security in a fixed daily routine. This leads us into the next section. For some prisoners, the experience of imprisonment can have a significant, detrimental impact on their psychological well-being, with some harming themselves or committing suicide in prison.

psychological health, self-harm and suicide in prison

The psychological health of prisoners has been assessed by numerous researchers. Some have considered psychological health under the umbrella term of adjustment to prison whereas others have used questionnaire-based measures such as the General Health Questionnaire. Researchers have reported levels of psychological distress that are concerning. For example, a study found that of a sample of UK female prisoners a third could be considered to be suffering from short-term psychiatric disorders. This proportion was much higher than the levels reported for the general public. Similarly, another study found with a sample of young offenders (aged 16–21) that over fifteen per cent were suffering from severe anxiety, twelve per cent severe depression, and thirty-eight per cent showed clinically high levels of hopelessness.

Similar figures were found by Jessica Woodhams and Susie Grennan. Around an eighth of our sample of male young offenders scored in the severe to extremely severe range for depression, anxiety and stress. With a sample of adult prisoners,

Jessica Woodhams found that over six per cent of prisoners reported levels indicative of clinical anxiety and depression. However, some caution should be exercised before drawing any firm conclusions about the apparently poorer psychological health of prisoners compared to the general public. The apparent poorer mental and physical health of inmates might relate to a disproportionate number of prisoners being people of lower socioeconomic status, which is also associated with poorer mental and physical health.

From research that has tried to determine the causes of poor psychological health in prisons, including studies mentioned above, a number of factors have been identified:

- Male gender
- Younger inmates
- Longer sentences
- Being at the start of a sentence
- Fear of violence
- Poor access to prison facilities (e.g. education)
- Environmental stress
- Poor access to support services
- Victimization
- Perceiving physical health as poor
- Concerns about external relationships/housing.

That a substantial minority of prisoners are suffering with poor psychological health is concerning and seems to stand in stark contrast to newspaper claims that prison is easy. Some prisoners seem to be finding the experience extremely difficult. This is further confirmed if we consider the rates of self-harm and suicide in prison.

Official statistics suggest that suicide rates are high in prisons and in juvenile detention centres. One study found that sixteen per cent of juveniles in detention centres reported previous deliberate self-harm and twenty-seven per cent reported thinking about attempting suicide in the past. This was a much higher rate than that reported by samples of juveniles in the general community. Similarly, a study of female prisoners found that sixteen per cent had considered self-harming, fifteen per cent had considered attempting suicide and six per cent had attempted suicide in the previous month.

When considering the reasons that prisoners give for attempting suicide there are some clear parallels with those regarding poorer psychological health. Some of the factors that have been reported to be associated with suicide in prison include:

- A psychiatric diagnosis
- Taking psychotropic medication
- A very violent index offence
- An actual or expected lengthy sentence
- Overcrowding
- Relationship problems/social isolation
- Being a remand prisoner
- Grief/bereavement
- Feelings of hopelessness/depression
- Homesickness
- Victimization by prisoners/prison staff
- A history of suicide attempts/threats.

It should be noted that there is some controversy about whether self-harming and suicide should be considered as being essentially the same behaviour. One study compared the factors associated with both. The reasons for committing or attempting suicide seemed more related to concrete events. In contrast, the reasons given by prisoners for self-harming included expressing or relieving emotion which seem related to more ongoing problems. Another study found poor peer relationships and a history of sexual abuse to be associated with deliberate self-harm. If there are differences between the triggers of suicide and those of self-harm, this suggests that they will each require different types of intervention. For example, suicidal prisoners with a psychiatric diagnosis could be provided with appropriate medication whereas prisoners who use self-harming as a way of coping could be taught alternative methods of coping. This is a question that future research could investigate.

coping with imprisonment

The material reviewed so far in this chapter has suggested that for at least a minority of prisoners, experiencing imprisonment can have profound negative effects. The research has also indicated that the prison environment is stress-inducing. Coping refers to the ways in which we deal with stress. Considering that prison is a stressful environment, this raises the question of how prisoners cope with this experience.

Some methods used by prisoners to cope with imprisonment have been alluded to above. They might deal with the fear of violence by being violent towards others or through harming themselves. Prisoners may also cope by withdrawing themselves from the prison culture by occupying themselves in jobs which take them away from the rest of the inmate population. Alternatively, prisoners might use litigation or formal grievance procedures to cope. Such activities might be helpful to prisoners because they are tension-reducing and allow prisoners to spend their time in what they perceive to be a constructive way. Other prisoners might use drugs or withdraw themselves psychologically. Some prisoners take the opposite approach and fill their time with various activities such as studying or taking physical exercise, which are again more constructive.

Some of these coping strategies we might perceive as adaptive whereas others appear more maladaptive. Because the prison environment is one which in some respects is quite unlike the outside world, the methods people use to cope in everyday life might be inappropriate in the prison environment. Similarly, methods that would be unsuccessful in the outside world might work well in the prison environment. What we in the outside world regard as maladaptive could well prove adaptive in the prison environment and vice versa. For example, in the outside world, when experiencing a new situation you might seek help from authority figures. In the prison environment, because of the inmate code, this could be a maladaptive strategy. In the outside world, responding aggressively to teasing or rumour-spreading may not be appropriate, however, in the prison, where being able to look after yourself is valued, this could be perceived as an adaptive strategy. With this in mind, there are clearly still some types of coping in both environments which would be described as maladaptive, such as self-harming.

With the view to helping prisoners cope better with the experience of being imprisoned, criminal psychologists have conducted research to assess the coping strategies used by prisoners. When talking about coping strategies the research has generally identified three distinct types:

1. Problem-focused or task-oriented coping which involves developing means or seeking means of dealing with the situation that is causing the stress.
2. Emotion-focused coping which involves the regulation of emotion and can involve thinking about the stressful situation in a different way.
3. Avoidance coping which involves the individuals avoiding what is causing them stress.

Research findings as to what coping strategies prisoners use have been very mixed. Researchers associated with the University of Barcelona have suggested that many prisoners use problem-focused strategies, and some use avoidance coping. In contrast, Jessica Woodhams and Susie Grennan found avoidance coping to be prevalent.

Not all types of coping are considered to be of benefit to the individual. Problem-focused coping and avoidance coping have been associated with better psychological health in prisons whereas emotion-focused coping has been associated with poorer psychological health. Other studies have found a relationship between avoidance and emotion-focused coping and psychological distress. Until more research is conducted it is difficult to draw any conclusions from these studies. However, researchers in this field should be mindful of the unique social conditions at play in the prison environment, which could ser-iously limit the potential use of different coping strategies.

social support

When most of us are having a stressful day we are likely to turn to others as a means of coping. The support we get from other people is called social support. Sidney Cobb has defined social support as the receipt of information from others that one is cared for and valued. Several different forms of social support exist. Practical support includes providing someone with material goods or useful advice and information. In the prison environment this might involve telling a fellow inmate which member of staff they need to speak to about visiting arrangements. Emotional support includes offering reassurance or providing a shoulder to cry on. Social support can come from different sources including family, friends and intimate partners. You might have someone you will go to when you need a solution to a problem, whereas you may go to someone else if you just want a sympathetic ear.

Non-custodial studies such as those conducted with health workers and students have demonstrated that social support can reduce psychological distress. In the prison environment, fostering social support would therefore seem to be a good way of addressing the psychological distress experienced by some prisoners. This raises the question of where prisoners can seek social support. In theory, they could seek support from prison staff (such as prison officers, or prison guards as they are also called, psychologists or the chaplain), fellow prisoners and their friends and family outside the prison. Some prisons have also set up schemes, such as the Listener Scheme, where inmates serving long sentences can be trained in listening and counselling skills. Such prisoners can offer confidential support to other prisoners.

However, this is all in theory. In reality because of some of the factors we have discussed above, such as the inmate code, one can see how it might be quite difficult for prisoners to access these sources of support. Prisoners have reported an unwillingness to approach prison officers for help, perhaps as a result of the inmate code, although some will seek practical support from officers. We could question how easy it is for prison officers to offer social support to prisoners, keeping in mind their potentially conflicting roles. Although prison officers must contain the prisoners, they must also protect them and may have a rehabilitative role. Prison officers, as well as prisoners, are exposed to the environmental stressors of prison on a daily basis and it is quite possible that the psychological and physical consequences of this might affect their ability to offer support to inmates.

With the enforced distance between prisoners and intimate partners and friends outside the prison, the briefness of prison visits and the potential breakdown of these relationships, prisoners may find that their only source of support is other prisoners. However, prisoners may be wary of seeking support from other inmates should they appear weak and leave themselves open to exploitation. Hence, they might also limit themselves to seeking practical forms of support from fellow inmates. If prisoners feel unable to seek social support from other prisoners and prison officers, schemes such as the Listeners Scheme could therefore be of great importance.

Despite these obstacles, several studies have indicated relationships between social support from these various sources and reduced psychological distress, self-harm and suicide in prison. However, there have also been conflicting findings and it is likely that the obstacles outlined above may go some way to explaining these inconsistencies.

Having considered the experience of prisoners in general, the last part of this chapter turns to consider the experiences of two particular populations of prisoner; women and prisoners serving life sentences.

the experience of female prisoners

According to the International Centre for Prison Studies, the percentage of prisoners who are women ranges from 26.6 % to 0 % depending on the country. In some countries, a substantial minority of the prisoner population will therefore be female.

With this in mind, you may find it surprising that, in comparison to male prisoners, little research has been conducted with women prisoners. Researchers have recently begun addressing this disparity. When considering how women experience imprisonment researchers have suggested that prison has a more negative effect on women than on men. This was concluded from their higher levels of psychological distress, which did not seem to be explained by environmental factors.

In 1997, Her Majesty's Chief Inspector of Prisons interviewed numerous female prisoners, the majority of whom reported that prison had had a negative effect on them. The explanations for this varied. Some explained that prison had merely taught them to be better criminals and increased their knowledge of committing crimes whereas others referred to their emotional feelings. For example, some women explained that imprisonment had resulted in them feeling very angry or depressed.

The belief that female prisoners suffer more than male prisoners might be, in part, explained by women's roles as mothers. The same 1997 study found that two-thirds of female prisoners were mothers. Similarly, the US Department of Justice found seventy-nine per cent of women prisoners were mothers and frequently they were single parents. Separation from their children was given as female prisoners' greatest concern along with maintaining contact with other family members, who might be caring for their children. In addition, women prisoners reported being worried about the health of relatives, about their children being taken into permanent social care and their finances. In another study, imprisoned mothers also reported concern about their child's care in their absence and whether their child would stop thinking of them as their mother. In line with these concerns, women prisoners who are mothers have been found especially to suffer from poor psychological health. Female prisoners who are mothers, rather than female prisoners in general, might therefore be at greater risk of psychological distress.

The paths by which women enter the criminal justice system also suggest reasons for why women prisoners suffer greater psychological distress. As outlined by the US Department of Justice, a substantial number of women prisoners enter prisons with histories of being physically and sexually abused. It is therefore quite likely that some women prisoners will not only already be suffering from psychological distress prior to incarceration but may also therefore be more vulnerable to negative imprisonment factors.

With regard to social support, in a survey of women prisoners Her Majesty's Chief Inspector of Prisons found that over fifty per cent of the women prisoners interviewed reported having received no help after being imprisoned. In particular, seventy-five per cent of those who were drug abusers reported receiving no help to overcome their addiction. Substance abuse seems to be a greater problem for women prisoners than it is for men, as reported by the US Department of Justice in 2005. Such findings are therefore a concern since women's offending is also more likely to be drug-related. It would thus seem important to aid women prisoners in overcoming their drug habits if we are to prevent them reoffending when released.

When comparing female and male prisoners some of the difficulties they experience appear to be quite similar, however, women's roles as mothers and primary caregivers appear to put them at greater risk of psychological distress. To reduce this distress as much as possible, prison regimes may need to be developed with women prisoners' roles as mothers in mind. For example, the US Department of Justice has suggested arranging visiting times that coincide with out-of-school hours to enable children to visit their mothers.

Another group of prisoners who also appear at greater risk are those serving a life sentence.

experiencing life imprisonment

Prisoners serving a life sentence are sometimes referred to as 'lifers'. To receive such a long sentence, the types of crimes they have committed are typically serious, for example, murder. Such crimes are less common than others and therefore the number of lifers in prisons reflects this. In England and Wales in 2003, nine per cent of all prisoners were serving a life sentence. Similarly, the Australian Bureau of Statistics reports that in Australia in 2004, four per cent of sentenced prisoners were serving a life sentence.

What is meant by 'life sentences' can vary between countries. In some it literally means that the individuals will be imprisoned for the rest of their lives: in other countries it can mean periods of imprisonment of more than ten years. The Home Office reported that in England and Wales in 1999 the average length of sentence served by lifers was 15 years.

Research with lifers has found that compared to short-term prisoners, lifers experience a different set of stressors. Whilst damage to external relationships might be a concern for most prisoners, lifers have the added concern of whether their relationships with those outside prison can last for the long period of incarceration. They may experience difficulty coping with the gradual deterioration of these relationships and, because of the high turnover of short-term prisoners, they can experience further problems in forming bonds inside the prison. Lifers have reported concerns about losing their sense of identity due to the enforced passivity of prison and the lack of personal control. The stability of their environment can also be a concern. The indeterminate nature of life sentences may well be particularly stressful for some life-sentence prisoners because it causes them uncertainty, which is precisely what they seek to avoid. A study of the reasons for suicide by life-sentence prisoners also highlighted a number of these concerns, including disrupted relationships, the reality of the long sentence and failed appeals against their sentences.

As with much of the research with prisoners, research findings about the psychological distress experienced by life-sentence prisoners is mixed. Her Majesty's Inspector of Prisons did find elevated levels of psychological distress amongst this population. However, the report made the good point that inflated levels of disturbance in this population might not be a result of imprisonment. Instead, psychological disturbance could have contributed to the types of crimes life-sentence prisoners have committed. In other words, the psychological disturbance existed before their imprisonment, rather than being a result of it. The guilt experienced by some prisoners relating to their offences might also affect their psychological well-being.

This raises the question of how criminal psychologists and other prison staff can help life sentence prisoners cope with their specific stressors. In relation to dealing with uncertainty, Her Majesty's Inspector of Prisons suggested that lifers require long-term projects to give them a sense of stability. Alternatively, taking up a job in the prison that offers responsibility can help. Considering the apparently elevated rate of psychological distress in this population, their mental health needs might be greater and provisions may need to be made for this.

conclusions

Psychology has been able to make a meaningful contribution to the understanding of the experience of being imprisoned. The unique physical and social environment in prison does seem particularly prone to causing stress. However, prisoners are individuals, and vary in the stressors they experience and how they try to cope with these. The prison environment also seems to limit the means by which prisoners can cope with stress. This is something researchers should be mindful of when making recommendations. Finally, we have seen that there are some populations of prisoners who suffer particular stressors: life-sentence prisoners and prisoners who are mothers. There are other vulnerable populations within the prison population who have not been considered here. However, it is hoped that this chapter has given you an insight into the psychological difficulties these individuals can face and the obstacles criminal psychologists and other prison staff may face when trying to help them.

recommended further reading

Biggam, F. H. and Power, K. G. (1997) Social support and psychological distress in a group of incarcerated young offenders. *International Journal of Offender Therapy and Comparative Criminology*, 41, 213–30.

Edgar, K., O'Donnell, I. and Martin, C. (2003) *Prison violence: The dynamics of conflict, fear and power.* Cullompton, UK: Willan Publishing.

Hobbs, G. S. and Dear, G. E. (2000) Prisoners' perceptions of prison officers as sources of support. *Journal of Offender Rehabilitation, 31,* 127–42.

Ireland, J. L. (2002) *Bullying among prisoners: Evidence, research and intervention strategies.* Hove: Brunner-Routledge.

Johnson, R. and Toch, H. (1982) *The pains of imprisonment.* Beverley Hills, CA: Sage Publications.

Lindquist, C. H. and Lindquist, C. A. (1997) Gender differences in distress: Mental health consequences of environmental stress among jail inmates. *Behavioral Sciences and the Law, 15,* 503–23.

Loucks, N. (2004) Women in prison. In J. R. Adler (ed.) *Forensic psychology: Concepts, debates and practice,* pp. 287–304. Cullompton, UK: Willan Publishing.

Parisi, N. (ed.) (1982) *Coping with imprisonment.* Beverley Hills, CA: Sage Publications.

Rokach, A. and Cripps, J. E. (1998) Coping with loneliness in prison. *Psychological Studies, 43,* 49–57.

Snow, L. (2002) Prisoners' motives for self-injury and attempted suicide. *The British Journal of Forensic Practice, 4,* 18–29.

Toch, H. (1992) *Living in prison: The ecology of survival.* Washington, DC: American Psychological Association.

the rehabilitation of offenders: what works?

introduction

What are your views on the rehabilitation of offenders? Do you think that it is possible to alter the behaviour of offenders? Should offenders be given the opportunity of rehabilitation? Can long-term offenders become law-abiding citizens through the use of treatment programmes or do you think that an offender will always be an offender? Do you think that the time and money spent on interventions with offenders is justified or a waste of precious resources?

It seems that most people hold their own, sometimes strong, views relating to how offenders should be dealt with following conviction for an offence. Some think that they should be punished and may make statements such as 'offenders should be locked up and the key thrown away'. Others, however, think that offenders should have an opportunity, if appropriate, to receive treatment aimed at altering their behaviour in an attempt to prevent future offending. Still other groups think that the access to rehabilitation should depend on the type and seriousness of the crime committed, the number of previous convictions or the extent of harm caused to the victim of the crime.

Whatever an individual's perspective on this debate is, over the last twenty years there has been a renewed confidence in offender rehabilitation amongst practitioners and policy makers, especially in the United Kingdom and North America. Nowadays there are numerous rehabilitative programmes which offenders may undertake during their period of imprisonment or while on a community-based sentence. According to UK Home Office figures, in 2004 in England and Wales, over 15,000 offenders completed a community based offending behaviour programme and over 8,000 a prison based programme, many of which are delivered and managed by criminal psychologists. The growth in the use of programmes over the last few years can be demonstrated by comparing these figures against those from 2001. Then only 1,385 offenders completed community based programmes – less than ten per cent of the number that completed such programmes a few years later.

As mentioned briefly in Chapter 1, criminal psychologists have been instrumental in the design, implementation, management and delivery of offending behaviour programmes to a range of different types of offenders within both prison and community settings. These professionals use the psychological techniques contained within the programme manuals to target the offenders' problem-solving, social and personal control skills. Criminal psychological research has shown that offenders tend to be lacking in such skills and there is an argument that it is these cognitive deficits that contribute to an offender's decision to partake in criminal activities. Therefore criminal psychologists use these rehabilitative programmes to provide offenders with the opportunity to develop their problem-solving and social skills, to reduce rigid thinking and impulsivity and to use these new skills in order to select alternatives to criminal behaviour.

Criminal psychologists have also been involved in the evaluation of the effectiveness of offending behaviour programmes. With the public show of confidence in these programmes from governmental agencies, it would be reasonable to assume that the evidence concerning their effectiveness is positive and concrete. The reality, however, is that much more needs to be known about programmes and their effectiveness. This topic is still at a relatively early stage of development. With such rapid and large-scale development and implementation of these programmes within some criminal justice systems, the research base is yet to catch up. Our 2004 report (see suggested further readings) of a large-scale research project in England and Wales has produced tentative answers to some important questions, however, still others remain unanswered and new ones are emerging. More research is needed to understand fully the psychological and behavioural effects of offending behaviour programmes on the individuals who are allocated to them.

This chapter will explore the issue of offender rehabilitation and provide insight into the ongoing debate surrounding the effectiveness (or not) of offending behaviour programmes. The chapter will also introduce the reader to some examples of programmes, how they operate and what the research literature says about their ability to reduce reoffending rates. In order to set the scene a historical perspective on the development of offender rehabilitation will first be provided.

the rehabilitative debate

As mentioned above, the last ten years have witnessed a huge growth in the industry relating to offending behaviour programmes, particularly in the UK and North America. For example, within England and Wales, the Crime Reduction Programme provided governmental funding for the development and implementation of programmes in the Prison and Probation Services. In the following five years, nineteen programmes were approved for national implementation within the Prison and/ or Probation Service. On the other side of the Atlantic, the Correctional Service of Canada (CSC) also showed its support for rehabilitative programmes through the development of an expert advisory group charged with informing the CSC about offending behaviour programmes and their effectiveness.

However, such confidence in rehabilitative work with offenders has not always been evident. In the 1970s, the consensus amongst the majority of researchers, practitioners and policy makers was that offender rehabilitation was not a feasible venture. After the rehabilitative focus of the 1950s and 1960s, the 1970s heralded a shift in political opinion away from the more liberal policy of offender treatment to more punitive and retributive policies involving harsher sentencing and regimes. The foundation of this view is often traced to the publication in 1974 of a review paper 'What works? Questions and answers about prison reform' (Martinson 1974) – the publication of which happened to coincide with the political shift to the right in both the UK and North America. The paper reviewed 231 studies of offender treatment and, despite up to forty-eight per cent of studies showing positive effects, concluded that offender treatment 'cannot overcome, or even appreciably reduce, the powerful tendency for offenders to continue in criminal behaviour'. Advocates of offender treatment and those working within the treatment services must have been dismayed when such statements surfaced during this period.

The proponents of offender intervention did not lie down and accept defeat. Publications from the late 1970s and early 1980s continued to demonstrate that some interventions, when provided to certain types of offenders, could produce reductions in reconviction. The impact of these usually small-scale evaluations on the debate was not great, however. Many of these studies suffered from problems with the way in which they were conducted, which limited the conclusions that could be firmly stated. The studies that perhaps created the greatest impact on the rehabilitative debate were instead the meta-analyses that came to prominence towards the end of the 1980s and into the 1990s. Meta-analysis is a technique that allows for the statistical combination of findings from a number of studies investigating the same cause (for example, the effectiveness of offender treatment) but may have differed in their methodology (for example, different types of offenders, length of treatment, mode of treatment and so on). The meta-analysis technique, therefore, allows for the combination of findings from different small studies into one statistic: the 'effect size'. This statistic, in this case, is a measure of the effect of treatment across all the studies entered into the analysis.

The application of this type of analysis to the large number of available small studies showed that the treatment of offenders can, under the right circumstances, provide positive results. In fact, the use of meta-analysis concluded not only an average positive effect across all interventions reviewed, but also made it possible to pick out those features of interventions that were most likely to produce positive results. For the first time it was possible to highlight those features of interventions that, if incorporated into new programmes, were likely to result in a positive treatment effect.

the emergence of evidence-based practice within offender treatment

Just as the 1974 review paper had set the agenda for the following decade of public policy in relation to offender treatment, the findings of the meta-analyses of the 1980s and 1990s breathed new life into the rehabilitative agenda. These reviews provided valuable information to programme developers and practitioners concerning the parts of programmes that the research showed as being effective. Programme developers were able to design new programmes which comprised solely of those elements that the evidence said were effective.

THE CORRECTIONAL SERVICES ACCREDITATION PANEL (CSAP)

Accreditation criteria

1. *Clear model of change backed by research evidence*: The programme should have a plan for altering offenders' behaviour (that has been shown by previous research to be effective) thus resulting in less criminal behaviour.
2. *Selection of offenders*: The programme should specify for which offenders it is intended, taking into account such factors as offence type and their risk of further reconvictions.

CSAP *(cont.)*

3. *Targeting of dynamic risk factors*: The programme should target criminogenic factors (those which are linked to offending behaviour) that need to be and are capable of change.

4. *Range of targets*: The programme should address a range of targets as evidence has shown this to be more effective. If a narrow focus is used this should be justified in light of the evidence.

5. *Effective methods*: The programmes should use those methods that have been shown to be more likely to work. Cognitive behavioural methods (those that focus on challenging individuals' thoughts and attitudes in order to alter their behaviours) have been shown to work well with a range of offenders but other methods can be used if there is evidence for these.

6. *Skills orientated*: The programme should teach the offenders skills which will help them live and work a crime free life.

7. *Sequencing, intensity and duration*: The timetable of the programme should match the targeted offenders' learning styles and abilities in order to produce maximum impact.

8. *Engagement and motivation*: The content and methods of teaching should ensure that the offenders' engagement and motivation is retained and built upon throughout the programme.

9. *Continuity of programmes and services*: The programme should be fully integrated into the offenders' sentence and supervision plan.

10. *Ongoing monitoring*: Monitoring procedures should ensure that the programme is supported and resourced in order to ensure that effectiveness is not undermined.

11. *Ongoing evaluation*: Evaluation should be built in to the programme in order to inform the ongoing development of the programme.

Adapted from Home Office (2005)

In order to facilitate this process in England and Wales (and now in other countries, such as Australia, which have since followed suit and developed similar systems to the one described here), the government's Crime Reduction Programme provided funding not only for the development of programmes, but also for the establishment of an accreditation system for these programmes. This system comprised a Joint Prison and Probation Accreditation Panel (now entitled the Correctional Services Accreditation Panel – CSAP) which was set up in order to ensure that programmes developed for offenders in prison and on probation were grounded in the best available research evidence of the day. From the results of the meta-analyses, the panel of international experts in offender rehabilitation drew up a set of criteria to which all future programmes should adhere. Only programmes that met these criteria were to be adopted and implemented by the Prisons and Probation Service for delivery to the offenders under their supervision. The box above summarizes the evidence-based criteria that the CSAP have adopted.

The development of these 'What Works' principles has inevitably been reliant on the conclusions of research studies. In this sense, our knowledge about what constitutes an effective intervention can only ever be as good as the standard of research that is conducted in this area. If the standard of the research is poor, then the conclusions may be incorrect and our knowledge base will contain errors.

As within most branches of psychology, there have been (and continue to be) debates concerning what constitutes the gold standard of treatment–outcome research. The UK Home Office has recently proposed that research adopting a randomized control trial design (RCT: offenders are randomly assigned to either the intervention or a no-intervention group and their outcomes compared) is the highest standard possible. However, even research incorporating the best methodological designs can suffer from other problems that could still result in poor quality research.

The number of participants utilized in the research is important, as the statistics employed to measure any effect brought about by participation in the programme are sensitive to the size of the sample under investigation. Studies with smaller samples of participants are therefore less likely to detect any effect of treatment (if indeed one exists). The author of a study with a small sample size that yields no detectable treatment effect may conclude that the treatment is ineffective and should therefore be discontinued. However, an alternative explanation could be that the sample size used in the research was not large enough to detect the treatment effect. The call to discontinue the treatment programme based on such small studies could therefore be premature. Large-scale research projects are needed.

The choice of which indicator of treatment success (or failure) to use is also an important consideration in this type of research (which is often called treatment–outcome research). Most research in this area uses reconviction (either 'reconvicted' or 'not reconvicted') as the measure by which treatment success or failure is evaluated. While this indicator is useful from a policy perspective, it is only an approximation of reoffending. Someone who completes a programme may have subsequently committed a dozen or more crimes but as he or she was not caught and reconvicted, it would appear that the programme was effective. Conversely, the programme could have reduced the severity or frequency of an individual's offending behaviour but the crude measure of reconviction would not detect this positive change. Some researchers have tried to counter these problems by utilizing self-report information from the individuals themselves or asking their family, friends and other associates about the individuals' behaviour. This type of research, however, can be time-consuming, expensive to conduct and is only ever as good as the accuracy of the reports received.

assessment of offenders

As mentioned above, it is clear from the research findings of the last twenty years or so that not all treatment programmes will reduce recidivism rates for all offenders, and that some programmes of rehabilitation may be more effective with certain types of offenders than with others. For example, it stands to reason that an offender who has been caught committing a residential burglary may not be responsive to a treatment programme which aims to address aggressive behaviour. If the burglar does not display aggressive behaviour, or if aggressive behaviour does not relate to his or her offending behaviour, then a programme with aggression as its main treatment target is not going to equip the burglar with the necessary skills to stop burgling homes.

Similarly, someone who has a long history of offending or has been convicted of a serious offence (such as a violent or sexual offence) may have different treatment needs from someone who has been caught committing an offence for the very first time. Those offenders who have made crime their way of life may only benefit from a more intense intervention which addresses a range of needs. Their behaviour may well be more engrained than that of the first time offender and hence a greater depth of behaviour modification is needed.

Finally, offenders who are illiterate or have good reason why they would not be able to cope in a treatment group setting may need a different type of treatment programme from those who perform well in groups and can read and write adequately. Likewise, female offenders may require different types of programmes from male offenders, and the needs of ethnic minority groups may again be different. These may range from requiring materials to be provided in their first language, to the programme needing to address cultural or religious issues which may impact on the process of treatment. For example, some ethnic minority groups may find it particularly difficult to talk about their criminal behaviour within a group setting.

The above factors have been conceptualized into the three principles of risk, need and responsivity of offender rehabilitation. In order for treatment to reach its maximum effectiveness, it should be appropriate for those individuals in attendance. Programmes are deemed appropriate if they adhere to three principles mentioned above. The following section will explore these principles in more depth and will assess how they are important when matching an offender to the right intervention.

the risk principle

The risk principle states that those offenders who are more likely to reoffend, or, in other words, are at a higher risk of reoffending, should receive a greater level or intensity of intervention than those who are at a lower risk of reoffending. The thinking behind this is that those who are lower risk are less likely to reoffend and hence are less likely to need an intervention to help them desist from crime. In contrast, those offenders who are high risk need some form of intervention in order to prevent future criminal behaviour. With a limited pool of resources, the risk principle states that intervention should be targeted towards those who are most likely to gain from it.

Herein lies the dilemma of the risk principle. In a recent evaluation of community-based offending behaviour programmes carried out by the Universities of Leicester and Liverpool in the UK, those offenders who failed to complete programmes and those who failed even to start the programmes were the very people who are judged by the risk principle to be in greater need of treatment. This research found that those who dropped out of treatment at that time were at a higher risk of reconviction than those who went on to complete it. Thus it would seem that not only is it necessary to target those individuals who are most in need of treatment, but it is also necessary to support such individuals through to successful completion of the programme. Further investigation needs to examine the reasons for non-completion, especially within high-risk groups. Once this evidence is available it will then fall to treatment services to ensure that their provision is adapted in line with these findings in order to achieve maximum levels of treatment completion.

the need principle

While the risk principle states that the duration or dosage of the treatment should be linked to the risk that the particular offender presents, the need principle states that the programme should address the criminogenic needs of the offenders that attend it. But what is meant by criminogenic needs?

It is often the case that offenders have problematic issues in many areas of their lives that need resolution in order to aid their desistence from crime. For example, they could be homeless, or have problems with their finances, or they may have relationship problems or substance use habits. Offenders may have low levels of educational ability or have problems getting and holding onto employment, or it may be that their associates (family and friends) are involved in crime. Offenders, then, can often present for treatment with a whole host of issues, or needs, that require addressing.

These needs can be classified into two different types: criminogenic and non-criminogenic. Criminogenic needs are those that are related to the individual's offending behaviour. It is these problems or issues that contribute to the individuals continuing in their pattern of criminal behaviour. Since these criminogenic needs are dynamic or theoretically changeable, treatment that focuses on the resolution of these problems is more likely to be associated with a reduction in recidivism.

To demonstrate this point an analogy can be drawn between an offender attempting to abstain from offending and a person who is attempting to abstain from smoking cigarettes. Smoking can be conceptualized as problem behaviour in much the same way as criminal behaviour can. It could be that both the smoker and the criminal see that their behaviour is having a detrimental effect on their lives and the lives of their loved ones. In addition, it could be that both individuals have tried to stop their problem behaviour but, while they may have managed to do so for a short time, eventually they have lapsed back into their old habits.

In order for smokers to give up smoking they will need to look at what is contributing to their continuing habit. It could be that their partner also smokes and encourages them to continue smoking or it could be that they use smoking as a way of controlling their weight by having a cigarette instead of eating. Just as smokers need to work out what it is about their circumstances that prevent them from giving up cigarettes, it is necessary for offenders and their case managers to assess what circumstances or issues within their lives are likely to be contributing to the continuation of their offending behaviour. It is these criminogenic needs that the treatment programme should address in order to attempt to alter the behaviour of those in attendance.

the responsivity principle

Just as the risk and need principles state that the offenders' risk and need status should be considered in the design of programmes and the allocation of offenders to them, the responsivity principle states that treatment programmes and the delivery of them should be geared to the offenders' abilities and learning styles. In the broadest sense this principle means that programmes based on cognitive behavioural principles (those that focus on challenging individuals' thoughts and attitudes in order to alter their behaviour) should be adopted as these have been shown by research to be most effective with offenders. This consideration has been termed 'general responsivity' as these methods, in a general sense, have been shown to produce positive results.

However, there is also a much wider interpretation of the responsivity principle which has been termed 'specific responsivity'. Specific responsivity refers to the need for interventions (and for those that deliver them) to be sensitive to the individual needs of those who are in attendance on the programme. The individual characteristics that should be considered under specific responsivity range from race and gender to cognitive and reading ability, motivation and the ability to function in groups. This list is not exhaustive and may include many other individual factors that should be addressed if it is felt that they may impact on the effectiveness of the intervention for that individual. For example, if an offender has a low reading ability and would struggle to complete some of the exercises within a programme because of this, then the service provider should be responsive to this and provide additional support for this offender.

As we have seen over the last few pages, there has been a shift over the last ten to twenty years towards the use of offender rehabilitation within some criminal justice systems. Nowadays, the design of programmes is becoming better rooted in research findings and increasingly practice is being based on the evidence that is available. However, there are still many questions to be answered about the effectiveness of programmes and research needs to build on what we already know in order to expand knowledge of 'What Works'.

offending behaviour programmes

This section will present two examples of offending behaviour programmes.

think first

Think First is a treatment programme which has been specially devised for offenders who are deemed to be medium to high risk of reoffending and have displayed a general pattern of offending, not specializing in any type of crime, in their past. The programme was designed by Professor James McGuire, a Forensic Clinical Psychologist in the UK, for use within the Prison and Probation Services of England and Wales but has also been adopted by some correctional services in Australia. The core of the Think First programme is a block of twenty-two group-based sessions, each of which is two hours long. In addition, offenders are expected to attend pre-group and post-group sessions which are not group-based but instead are delivered on a one-to-one basis.

Think First is a programme built upon cognitive behavioural principles. It therefore aims to address offenders' attitudes and underlying thought processes that contribute to offending behaviour. The principle goal of the programme is to help those who attend the programme to acquire, practise and begin to use a number of problem-solving and related skills that will allow them to manage their lives and any associated difficulties in a more appropriate manner and without resorting to offending.

For example, offenders (generally speaking) tend to be rigid in the responses they choose in certain problem circumstances. For example, if a male offender is in a bar and catches another male (a stranger) looking at them, it may be the case that the offender thinks that the other male is goading them or 'offering them out'. The offender's response may be to do what he always does when someone is acting that way towards him – he goes over and punches the other male. If the offender had stopped to weigh up the situation, he may have found that the stranger was not actually staring at him but was eyeing up the attractive female behind him! The offender has, therefore, not only impulsively jumped to the wrong conclusion about why the man is looking in his direction, but has also stuck rigidly to his usual course of action for resolving such circumstances. The question the programme asks of the offender is – is there an alternative action that could have been taken to remedy the situation in a more pro-social way?

Rigid thinking is just one factor that may contribute to offenders committing a crime such as this assault described above. Think First aims to teach the offender alternative responses by providing such skills as problem awareness, problem definition, information gathering, distinguishing facts from opinions, alterative solution thinking, consequential thinking, selection and decision-making and perspective taking. The programme also highlights the need for self-management in situations such as the one outlined above and provides skills to enhance personal control over the feelings and behaviours that may cause problems for offenders. The programme also uses training in how to interact in social situations ('social interaction training') and 'values education' (or moral reasoning) training in order to strengthen the offenders' social problem-solving skills.

Evaluations of the programme, to date, have provided tentatively positive evidence for its rehabilitative qualities. An initial evaluation of the programme, conducted by researchers at the University of Liverpool, found positive pre- to post-programme changes on psychometric tests measuring constructs such as attitudes towards offending, anticipation of reoffending, victim empathy and impulsivity.

A number of reconviction studies of the programme have also been performed by two groups of researchers in the UK: one group from the Probation Studies Unit at the University of Oxford and another from the Universities of Leicester and Liverpool. Both research groups reported significant reductions in the reconviction rates of those who completed the programme compared to those who failed to complete. However, the use of those who failed to complete programmes (or non-completers) as a comparison group is not ideal. Both groups of researchers have shown that the non-completers were already at a higher risk of reconviction than those who managed to complete. It stands to reason that those who are at a higher risk of reconviction are more likely to be reconvicted.

The research carried out by the Universities of Leicester and Liverpool, therefore, also compared those who completed the programme with a comparison group of similar individuals who had received an alternative community sentence. When holding the effects of age, risk of reconviction, gender and offence type constant, completers of the programme were almost thirty percent less likely to be reconvicted compared to the non-completers and the comparison group.

A finding common across these evaluations, however, is the high non-completion rate of programmes (this is common to all community programmes and not just Think First). Non-completion rates for Think First ranged from 62 to 72 per cent of those who were ordered by the courts to attend the programme. Although there are indications that these figures have improved since the research was conducted, these findings have to raise questions about whether the delivery of programmes can be enhanced in order to persuade more offenders to complete.

aggression replacement training

The Aggression Replacement Training programme (ART) is similar in many respects to Think First – it provides specific cognitive behavioural exercises which aim to develop offenders' thought processes and attitudes in relation to crime and criminal behaviour. The ART programme differs from Think First and other general offending programmes in that it is an offence-specific programme – this means that it is targeted at a specific group of offenders. As the name would suggest, the ART programme is aimed at offenders who have displayed violent offending or aggression related problem behaviour.

ART was originally designed by the late Professor Arnold Goldstein in the USA for use with juvenile offenders but has since spread geographically and is now delivered to offenders across North America as well as in countries such as the UK, the Netherlands and Sweden. Additionally the contents of the programme, originally developed for work with children and adolescents, have also been adapted for use with adult and mentally disordered offenders.

The ART programme consists of three component parts. Each group session comprises two of these components and these are rotated throughout the programme so that an equal amount of each component is received. The three components are skill-streaming, anger control training and moral reasoning training: each of these will now be explained in more detail.

Skillstreaming is the behavioural part of the programme. Based on the understanding that offenders characteristically lack personal, interpersonal and social cognitive skills, the skillstreaming element is designed to teach the offenders these skills and provides the opportunity to practise and rehearse these skills. The provision of constructive feedback helps the offenders to transfer their learning into real-life situations.

Anger control training constitutes the emotion-based branch of the programme. This component addresses the emotions of offenders and how these relate to their ability to control (or not!) their anger. Anger control training does just that – it teaches offenders anger control techniques. The aim of this section of the programme is to provide offenders with alternative courses of action in situations where their anger would have previously resulted in violence and offending.

The moral reasoning section of the programme provides offenders with the chance to challenge their attitudes towards certain situations. While the other components are thought of as the behavioural and affective elements, the moral reasoning component is the thinking element. This section of the programme provides moral dilemmas which build in their complexity throughout the programme. The aim of these dilemmas is to challenge the reasoning of those in attendance on the programme and to help them choose appropriate skills for the situations that they may find themselves in.

The ART programme has been subject to a relatively large number of evaluation studies to test its effectiveness. Across geographical locations and different client groups such as incarcerated juvenile delinquents, community-based youths and their families, juvenile gang members and adults, several promising findings have indicated the potential effectiveness of the ART programme. Evaluations have reported cognitive gains in line with the programme aims, as well as more behavioural outcomes such as reduced re-arrest rates, reduced reconviction and enhanced community functioning. Other research, however, has presented mixed results – for example, improvements in the cognitive functions that ART targets but no transference of these gains into behavioural change. As ever, further research is needed to unpick the research findings in relation to the ART programme.

conclusions

The aim of this chapter was to provide an overview of the 'What Works' debate and the current state of the field of offender rehabilitation. The chapter started out by asking what your thoughts were about the rehabilitation of offenders. Have they changed at all in light of the contents of this chapter?

Rather than focus on the ethical and moral question of whether an offender deserves the chance of rehabilitation, this chapter has focused on the issue of whether treatment is effective and has explained how today's practices are becoming based within evidence-based practice, at least in some countries. The chapter has also provided a couple of examples of the programmes along with the related research evidence.

It is hoped that the general message taken from this chapter is that the rehabilitation of offenders may be successful for certain individuals and under certain conditions. However, there are still many unanswered questions – for example, how can we ensure that a greater proportion of offenders complete programmes? Why do people drop out from programmes? Are the right individuals targeted for the programmes? Could altering the dosage of these programmes increase the treatment effect? And so on ... More research is needed to try and unpick the answers to questions such as these.

recommended further reading

Goldstein, A. P., Nensen, R., Daleflod, B. and Kalt, M. (2004) *New perspectives on aggression replacement training.* Chichester: John Wiley.

Hollin, C. R. (ed.) (2003) *The essential handbook of offender assessment and treatment.* Chichester: John Wiley.

Hollin, C. R., Palmer, E. J., McGuire, J., Hounsome, J., Hatcher, R., Bilby, C. and Clark, C. (2004) *Pathfinder programmes in the Probation Service: A retrospective analysis.* Home Office Online Report 66/04. Available at http://www.homeoffice.gov.uk/rds/pdfs04/rdsolr6604.pdf.

Home Office (2005) *What Works: Accreditation – a summary.* Accessed 25 July 2005 at http://www.crimereduction.gov.uk/workingoffenders13.htm.

McGuire, J., Mason, T. and O'Kane, A. (2000) Effective interventions, service and policy implications. In J. McGuire, T. Mason and A. O'Kane (eds) *Behaviour, crime and legal processes,* pp. 289–314. Chichester, UK: Wiley.

McGuire, J. (ed.) (1995) *What Works: Reducing reoffending: Guidelines from research and practice.* Chichester, UK: John Wiley.

Martinson, R. (1974) What works? Questions and answers about prison reform. *The Public Interest 35*: 54.

online resources

http://www.crimereduction.gov.uk/workingoffenders1.htm
This is a UK Home Office web site related to crime reduction issues which contains information on the What Works movement.

the management and treatment of sex offenders

This chapter will look at how criminal psychology helps us understand some of the reasons why men and women become sex offenders and how sex offenders are punished, treated and managed once they are caught. The chapter will also talk about the effectiveness of these treatments; do the punishments work? Do they stop sex offenders committing crimes once they are let out of prison?

Sex offending is thought of as a very serious problem within contemporary society. It is an offence that seems to be more than just a crime; it is regarded as a social and health problem and is frequently reported in newspapers and on the television and radio. Sex offending in the UK includes crimes such as rape (penetration by the penis of someone's vagina, anus or mouth without consent); assault by penetration (penetration by a body part or object of someone's vagina or anus without consent); sexual assault (sexual touching); administering a substance with intent to commit a non-consensual sexual act (this covers spiking someone's drink); sexual activity with a child (under the age of sixteen), causing or inciting a child to engage in sexual activity; engaging in sexual activity in the presence of a child; meeting a child following sexual grooming (this new offence has been triggered by child abusers using the Internet to meet children); abusing positions of trust (it is unlawful for people who work with children, say in youth services, care homes or schools, to have sex with anyone in their care who is under the age of eighteen).

The National Society for the Prevention of Cruelty to Children (NSPCC) reports that one in six children are sexually abused before the age of sixteen and that children are far more likely to be abused by someone they know (a family member or a neighbour) than by a stranger. Other research has shown that one in four women have been subject to a sexual assault or rape. In England and Wales in the period 2004–5 there were 60,000 sexual crimes recorded by the police. This was an increase on the previous year by 8,000 crimes, but in this period the Sex Offences Act 2003 came into force meaning that new offences, such as grooming and abuse of trust, were taken into account. A higher crime rate might also partly be an increase in the reporting of sexual offences, which implies that people are becoming more intolerant of unacceptable behaviour and believe that reported offences will be taken seriously by the police and courts. In the USA, the country that puts more of its population in prison than any other country in the world, almost one quarter of the state prison populations are sex offenders. Despite this, rates of sexual offending are very much lower than for almost every other type of crime and criminal psychologists question whether our fear of sexual offending has been heightened by the constant media discussion on the topic.

Research carried out on adult sexual offenders has shown that the majority say that they started to sexually offend before the age of eighteen, and studies of adolescent sexual offenders indicate that the majority commit their first sexual offence before fifteen years of age and not infrequently before twelve years of age. A trend consistent across the literature is that approximately twenty per cent of sexual offences are committed by adolescents. However, in England and Wales sexual offences account for less than one per cent of all crimes committed by young people aged ten to seventeen that actually result in them being put in a secure institution or being under the supervision of youth offending services. Males account for ninety-eight per cent of convicted sexual offenders (Youth Justice Board, 2004). This high proportion may be an indication that people still find it difficult to believe that women can be sex offenders too.

Victim surveys, for example the 2005 British Crime Survey (Nicholas *et al.*, 2005), show higher levels of sex offending than are reported to the police and it is commonly accepted that there is a high proportion of hidden sexual victimization. The human and financial cost of sexual offending to victims and the social and health services is large, as is the public investment in policing, prosecuting and incarcerating sex offenders.

Crime prevention policies always seem to be heavily influenced by media and public pressure, and sexual offending has thus become a major challenge for social policy. How can the government and policy-makers make sensible, evidence-based decisions about how to deal with sex offenders, while meeting the demands of the public? It is clear that media reporting of sexual offending is often distorted, for example, giving the impression that young women are very likely to be sexually attacked on the way home from a night out, or that young boys will be abused by strangers. Exaggerating the danger that sexual offenders pose is problematic and can increase public fear, stigmatize and hinder rehabilitation of offenders who have changed their lifestyles.

MEGAN'S LAW AND THE CAMPAIGN FOR SARAH'S LAW

Megan Kanka was a seven-year-old girl who was raped and murdered by a convicted sex offender in 1994 in New Jersey, USA. Three months after her murder the State of New Jersey passed the first version of Megan's Law. This stated that when sex offenders are released into the community, that community will be 'actively notified' of their presence. If the offenders are assessed as being 'medium risk' of reoffending, then schools and community groups that may encounter those offenders will be notified. If the offenders are assessed as being at 'high risk' of reoffending, then schools, community groups and members of

MEGAN'S LAW *(cont.)*

the public, such as neighbours, will be notified. Active notification means that leaflets are sent out, people are visited by their
local police, e-mails are sent to schools and community groups,
and notices may be placed in local newspapers. The Federal version of Megan's Law, which was passed in May 1996, signed by
President Clinton, is different. This law requires States to
release information to the public about offenders, but it does
not require them to 'actively notify' the public. This means that
information about offenders' names and addresses is made
accessible to the public in listings at criminal justice agencies,
registry books, or electronic formats (for example, on some
police Internet sites). If a state does not make this information
available, then crime prevention funding is withheld from the
state. As well as collecting information on adult sex offenders,
twenty-eight states have a register for juvenile sex offenders
and of these twenty-one release information on these offenders to
the public.

Advocates of Megan's Law believe that active community
notification will help criminal justice agencies in investigations, establish legal grounds to hold known sex offenders,
deter sex offenders from committing future crimes and offer the
public information that they can use to protect their children
from offenders.

From www.megans-law.net

In the UK a campaign for a similar law came from the *News of
the World* newspaper and the parents of Sarah Payne, who was
killed in 2001. However, the Home Secretary (the government
minister who deals with law and order) at the time was not con-
vinced that public access to information on the Sex Offender
Register would be helpful in protecting children. A senior police
officer stated that 'Sarah's Law' would drive offenders underground, which would then stop criminal justice agencies from
monitoring their movements or treating them.

In the USA, such concerns led to Megan's Law in 1996, which allows private and personal information on those registered as sex offenders against children, to be made available to the community (see the box on the previous pages for more information). In the UK, the Sexual Offences Act 2003 includes substantial increases in sentence length for many sexual offences and increased management of offenders for up to ten years after a sentence has been spent.

how is a sexual offender defined?

It is very difficult to give a full and complete definition of a sexual offender – examples might include someone who has committed a sexual offence, someone who has been convicted of a sexual offence or someone who has committed a sexual act without the consent of the other person. Consent might not have been given for a number of reasons. The victims might have withheld it, or they might not have been in a position to give consent to the sexual act (for example, they might be under the age of consent, be mentally disabled, drunk, drugged or unconscious). Researchers have suggested that there are two types of sexual offence, the sexually aggressive act – which is a non-consensual act – and a breach of a sexual taboo. Breaches of taboo are sexual behaviours that have taken place between two consenting adults but which are against the law, for example, in some states in the USA oral and anal sex are sexual offences, even if taking place in a consensual relationship.

what causes sexual offending?

There is no single cause of sexual offending and our understanding of what makes someone a sexual offender is far from perfect. There are a number of different ways in which sexual offending has been explained. These include:

- *Developmental histories.* Studies on this topic compare the childhood and development of sex offenders with non-sexual offenders. They try to find out what the differences are in the histories of these people, which will then, hopefully, show whether there is a childhood trigger for sexual offending.

- *Comparisons of adult activity and functioning.* Again, these types of studies compare sexual offenders with non-offenders, but they try to find out what it might be in adult functioning that causes sexual offending.
- *Risk prediction studies.* These studies tend to look at sex offenders only, and try to see what part of adult functioning is linked to repeat offending. Are there aspects of a person's perception, intuition, thought processes or ability to reason that makes them at a higher risk of re-offending than someone else, and what are these aspects?
- *Descriptive models of the offence process.* These studies look at what happens in the run up to an offence, while the offence is taking place and after the offence.

Studies that have compared childhood experiences of sexual offenders with non-offenders have identified key factors which may be related to sexual offending. The first key theme is the relationship between children and their parents. This relationship is likely to be the blueprint for all future relationships; so if this relationship is marked by untrustworthiness and lack of caring, then so too will all future relationships. Building on this, other researchers have found that sex offenders showed poorer relationships with their parents than did non-offenders. They found that abusers of children within their own family (intra-familial offenders) were very likely to report poor relationships with their mothers, saying that they were abusive, unloving or uncaring. Rapists reported that their fathers were uncaring. As with other types of offenders, sex offenders often have parents who were lawbreakers. Living in a family where anti-social behaviour is the norm is reported to hinder a child's moral and social development, and is likely to lead lives where crime plays a significant part.

When trying to understand why sex offenders commit offences, people often ask whether it is true that all sex offenders were abused as children. While it is unlikely that all sex offenders *were* abused as children, there is research evidence to show that a significant proportion were – around a quarter of rapists and almost two-thirds of child abusers according to one study. Rapists report very high levels of physical abuse from their fathers and intra-familial offenders are more likely to have been physically abused as children than their non-offending peers. However, when considering this sort of information, one needs to think about how it was gathered. Most of it comes from self-report questionnaires and most of the abuse was not reported at the time. This is not surprising, given that we know abuse of any kind at the hands of family members is severely under reported. Recently, research has shown that offenders reporting sexual abuse in earlier life drops from seventy per cent to twenty per cent when a polygraph (sometimes known as lie a detector) is employed. (For more on the polygraph see chapter 4.)

Some of the developmental experiences mentioned above are often typical of many types of offenders, not just sex offenders. So it is important to think about what it is that separates sex offenders from people who are sometimes termed 'general offenders'. Researchers have suggested that some form of salient sexual experience may, when coupled with other developmental issues, set a person on a path to sexual offending. Early exposure to pornography is one such experience which has been studied; one study showed that twenty-two per cent of sexual offenders were exposed to pornography before the age of ten compared to two per cent of non-sexual offenders. Pornography typically supports a view of sex as being focused on one person's pleasure, which might lead to a selfish approach to sexual behaviour. For example, a teenage boy may find that an arousing experience may fuel future masturbatory fantasies in which he is in control and powerful, something which is at odds with the rest of his life. These fantasies can spill into interpersonal relationships and lead to future offending.

We have considered some developmental issues that might influence people becoming sex offenders, but there are also explanations of sexual offending behaviour which look at adult functioning. It is generally assumed that all sexual offenders have deviant sexual interests, but this is not the case. Some sex offenders do show arousal to deviant forms of sexual behaviour, but just as many show arousal to non-deviant stimuli. More recent research shows that deviant fantasies are linked to mood, with this type of fantasy being used to rid the offender of anger, boredom or humiliation. This is supported by work which shows that sex offenders use sex as a coping strategy more regularly than non-sexual offenders.

Sex offenders, especially child abusers, seem to have difficulty in developing and maintaining intimate adult relationships. They find it difficult to express affection, give support or resolve arguments, and are often overly sensitive to rejection. They seem to want intimacy with another adult, but are fearful of it and, perhaps because of this dilemma, they often enter into adult relationships impulsively. This impulsivity also tends to be seen in other aspects of the offenders' lives, so an inability to stay organized or have control over impulses are seen as being predictors of risk of offending. Linked to this seems to be offenders' inability to cope with stressors in their lives. They have poor coping mechanisms which means that they do not deal well with the little problems that life throws at them, and research has shown that subjective distress, namely anger, anxiety, depression or boredom, is often a precursor to offending. When trying to cope with everyday life, sexual offenders seem to have distorted or dysfunctional thinking styles towards certain things. For example, if the female partner of a rapist had not managed to cook a meal on time, the offender might put this down to his partner stopping him from going out with his friends which would be humiliating for him and would suggest that she was trying to control him. This form of thinking, termed as 'hostile masculinity', tends to over value traditional male behaviour (dominance and power) and under-values female traits, such as gentleness. Distorted thinking patterns for child molesters include beliefs that children are interested in sex or are knowledgeable about sex.

It was noted above that work has also been conducted on describing patterns of behaviour in sexual offenders. Below are patterns of behaviour for male child abusers, (although this model would probably fit for female offenders too). This is a four-step model in which each step has to be carried out before the offender moves on to the next one.

THE FOUR-STEP MODEL OF SEXUAL OFFENDING

Step One – motivation to abuse

According to the model, there are three reasons why offenders might want to abuse children: being sexually aroused by a child; feeling emotional intimacy with a child; or wanting to have sex with an adult, but being unable to.

Step Two – overcoming internal inhibitors

We all have inhibitions about certain things in our lives. Think about whether you would be able to get up and sing in public, complain about poor service in a restaurant or ask someone you had only just met out on a date. What would it take to get over these inhibitions? A gin and tonic or a pint of lager or a bit of self-talk to give your confidence a boost, perhaps. The same thing is true of child abusers: they need to overcome their internal inhibitions, but these inhibitions are about abusing children. They often use alcohol, drugs or manage to generate excuses or justifications (cognitive distortions) to help them believe that the abuse is acceptable.

Step Three – overcoming external inhibitors

At this stage the offender needs to look for opportunities to offend. These might be offering to babysit, changing sleeping arrangements in a home or arranging to meet a child via the Internet. This stage is all about trying to be alone with the potential victim.

Step Four – overcoming the victim's resistance

Clearly the abuser has to ensure that the child complies with the abuse. There are at least two ways in which this is achieved. The first is through threats ('If you tell, your mum won't believe you and you'll be put in care') or violence, and the second is through what is termed 'grooming'. This is where an offender offers bribes to a child. These bribes might be material – sweets, presents or treats – or emotional – offering a 'shoulder to cry on'.

This model has been very influential and is often used in treatment programmes as a tool to help the offenders talk through their offending behaviour and to change this behaviour.

offender treatment

In this section the treatment, supervision and management of sex offenders will be discussed. It will cover how offenders are selected for treatment and what that treatment consists of, and will also talk about how effective the treatments are at reducing reoffending. The supervision of offenders once they have been released from prison will also be covered.

In several countries, offenders are no longer left in prison without considering the nature of their offence. The thinking behind sex offender rehabilitation has changed along with the development of general offender rehabilitation programmes (as discussed in chapter 10). Since the early 1990s, when offenders are sentenced to a prison stay or a community penalty in the UK they are also assessed for whether they are suitable to take part in a Sex Offender Treatment Programme (SOTP). There are a number of methods for discovering whether offenders are suitable and if they are, what risk level of committing another sexual offence they present. In English prisons Thornton's Structured Risk Assessment (SRA) is often used to see what level of risk an offender presents before treatment. This procedure looks at what are termed 'dynamic risk factors'. These are psychological factors, which affect beliefs and behaviour, and are possibly changeable. The SRA looks at four factors:

1. *Sexual interests* – this is concerned with the preoccupation the offenders have with sex (for example, whether they have a 'preference' for rape or sex with children) and offence-related fetishes.
2. *Distorted attitudes* – this examines the distorted thinking of the offenders. Do they see women as untrustworthy or manipulative? Children as sexual beings?
3. *Socio-affective functioning* – this looks at how offenders fill emotional needs. Do they prefer intimacy with children rather than adults? Are they aggressive and unemotional in their relationships?
4. *Self-management* – this considers how offenders manage their lives. Are they impulsive? Can they solve problems effectively?

One can clearly see here how this risk assessment tool is using the research reviewed earlier in this chapter about offenders' behaviour. Once an offender has completed a questionnaire it is scored by a psychologist who will then, after consideration of this and other documentation, decide what risk the offender presents and which set of programmes are most appropriate to deal with the offender's behaviour. Once an offender has completed a programme, the questionnaire is repeated to see whether the treatment programme has been effective in changing attitudes and behaviour.

The programmes being run in English and Welsh prisons and probation areas are only suitable for offenders whose level of intelligence is within the normal range. For offenders with a learning disability there is a specially adapted programme which employs exercises where cartoons and drawings are used.

The majority of treatment programmes used in the criminal justice system in the UK and many in the US, Canada, Australia and New Zealand are based on cognitive behavioural principles. This means that the programmes try to change the thinking patterns of offenders, their attitudes and perceptions. Once thought processes are changed, offenders are encouraged to change their patterns of behaviour from unacceptable and illegal to socially acceptable. Early treatments for sex offenders tended to be based on approaches found in Hans Eysenck's work in the 1950s, with much of this work being based on 'aversion therapy'. This meant that offenders were encouraged to think about an unacceptable fantasy until arousal, at which point an electric shock or nausea-inducing drug was administered. It was believed that the offender, after time, would associate the (deviant) sexual arousal with the unpleasant effect, which would then stop the offender from thinking these thoughts, and indeed evaluations of this work showed that reoffending rates were reduced. It was not until the 1970s that research on cognitive processes was included in the treatment of sexual offenders, and combinations of behavioural and cognitive research are often a very subtle and sophisticated mix of activities and approaches.

Researchers in North America have developed a list of what they term 'offence-specific' targets that an effective cognitive behavioural treatment (CBT) programme will cover. Offence-specific targets are patterns of thought which have been shown in research to be connected with sexually abusive behaviour and sexual offending.

offence specific targets

low self-esteem

Psychological research has shown that people low in self-esteem have characteristics which are similar to sexual offenders. They lack empathy, divert blame for their problems away from themselves, frequently experience negative emotions, handle stress poorly, engage in cognitive distortions and have poor relationship skills. People with poor self-esteem do not do well in treatment programmes, because they do not believe that they themselves are capable of changing. They tend to give up easily and 'fail' at the sight of small obstacles. If you are trying to treat sex offenders who display many of these attributes, then it makes sense to try and improve their sense of self-worth first so that you can maximize their potential to change.

cognitive distortions

Offenders distort incoming information or hold twisted views and beliefs. For example, child abusers may believe that children welcome their attention or rapists may believe that women are excited by forced sexual contact. These views help the offenders to justify their behaviour or minimize their guilt. Cognitive distortions also include denial, something which many sex offenders display – sixty-six per cent of child abusers and over half of rapists. They simply do not believe that they have committed a crime. It is very difficult to treat sex offenders effectively if they do not believe that they have done anything wrong, so many of the programmes include work to try and get the offenders to realize/accept this.

empathy deficits

Empathy is about being able to recognize distress and discomfort in others, to be able to understand the distress from the other person's perspective and then to experience compassion for the other person. Sex offenders tend to lack the ability to be empathic. One researcher suggests that sex offenders only lack empathy towards their own victims, with rapists being able to show empathy towards women in general, and child abusers being able to show empathy towards children in general (Hanson, 1997). This is why the majority of CBT programmes contain some work in victim empathy.

problems in social functioning

Many sex offenders have trouble in maintaining relationships with people. As offenders are not easily able to form relationships, this leads to loneliness which, in turn, leads to aggression and abusive behaviour. Offenders are taught, through role-play, how to overcome anxiety about making friendships, and engaging in conversation, and how to be assertive (rather than aggressive). They are shown how to respond in social situations and to gauge the behaviour of other people appropriately.

poor coping skills

Many offenders, not just sexual offenders, are unable to cope with stress and difficult life situations. With sex offenders, as mentioned above, the coping skills that they employ often mean that they use sexually inappropriate behaviour as a method of making themselves feel better and more in control of situations. Offenders are given examples of situations that they might come across and are encouraged to think about how they would deal with them. This element of the programme is important, especially when related to elements of programmes which deal with preventing reoffending, a concept known as relapse prevention.

aberrant sexual preferences

Dealing with deviant sexual preferences has been reduced as a component of treatment programmes, as not all offenders show deviant fantasies when they are initially assessed. Therefore, changing deviant preferences is only attempted when this is shown at assessment.

Despite the fact that there is little empirical evidence to show the effectiveness of covert sensitization, which is a method used to deal with deviant sexual behaviour, it is often still used in treatment. Most commonly covert sensitization means that an offender is asked to change the content of masturbatory fantasy to, for example, having sex with a consenting adult. For some offenders their desire for deviant sexual practices is so strong that drugs are sometimes used to contain them. Anti-androgens, which reduce the body's production of testosterone, are used but these do interfere with the body's normal hormonal functioning. There has also been more recent research on the effectiveness of SSRIs (serotonin reuptake inhibitors), which has found that they give offenders a feeling of greater control over their sexual preferences.

planning to prevent reoffending

A strategy to stop people from reverting to previous, negative behaviour, whether it is smoking, eating too much or too little, or offending, is called relapse prevention. Relapse prevention aims to serve two purposes: to integrate all of the aspects learnt on the programme and to develop strategies for maintaining the treatment-induced changes. This involves teaching offenders to avoid situations which might be problematic (for example being left alone with children) and to get them to think through how they will use the methods they learnt during the treatment programme.

CBT programmes also address behaviour and thought patterns that can, but do not always, have an influence on offending. These patterns are called 'offence-related targets', and can include anger and violence problems, substance (including alcohol) abuse and inadequate problem-solving. Addressing these problems might help an offender in leading a crime free life.

programmes in the criminal justice system (cjs) in england and wales

Prisons and probation areas in England and Wales run treatment programmes for sex offenders. Programmes in prisons are for offenders who have been sentenced for a sexual offence as their index, or main, offence or have committed a crime where there was a sexual element (for example for someone who has committed a murder but who raped the victim first). Offenders who take part in programmes within the community are sex offenders who have been sentenced to a Community Order with a requirement to attend a programme. Offenders who have been released from prison on licence are also sometimes required to attend treatment in the community at their probation office. These programmes are accredited by the Home Office, which means they meet a set of specified criteria to ensure that they are run properly in appropriate accommodation by trained professionals (psychologists, prison officers, probation officers and programme facilitators) and are subject to evaluation. The work of the programme leaders is monitored by a Treatment Manager who makes sure that the programmes are run properly, that leaders speak to the offenders with respect and that all offenders take part in the work undertaken in groups. The information that the Treatment Managers gather is then used to help the leaders develop their skills and is also routinely sent to the Home Office for monitoring.

The main programme delivered in prisons is called the Core programme. It includes work on distorted thinking, coping strategies, encouragement of engaging in normal sexual activity with a consenting adult, understanding offending, the costs and gains of offending, victim empathy and future life goals, skills and strategies. Programmes are run in groups, typically of ten to twelve offenders, and should be led by at least two facilitators, hopefully one man and one woman. It is important to have men and women to run programmes as they are able to show men and women working well together and showing respect for one another, something which is especially important for rapists in the group to see. The programme is delivered in eighty-six two-hour sessions, which are run about twice a week. Offenders are also required to complete 'homework' which builds on the things that they have learnt during the sessions. Homework has to be completed for an offender to 'pass' the programme. If offenders finish the programme a long time before they are due for release, they may be required to complete a Booster programme which goes over the things they have learnt again. The Prison Service also runs programmes for low risk offenders, high-risk offenders and also for offenders with learning difficulties.

Within the community programmes based on cognitive behavioural principles with offence-specific targets are also run. Again these are for groups of ten to twelve offenders and should be led by a mixed gender team. The initial phase of the programme is made up of sessions totalling fifty hours of treatment. Some offenders may leave the programme at this stage and others, with a higher risk, have to attend the remainder or part of the remainder of the 200 hours. In prison it is difficult for offenders to drop out of a programme, but in the community they can choose not to turn up more easily. However, offenders are mandated to take part in the programme as part of their sentence and if they miss or are late to two sessions without an acceptable excuse they are deemed to have breached their community sentence and are sent back to court for resentencing, which might mean a custodial (i.e. prison) sentence. If offenders' orders come to an end before the end of the programme they are at liberty not to finish the programme, which may have a negative impact on their reoffending.

do the programmes work?

Despite the fact that there has been a growth in the work conducted on sex offenders and treatment programmes, there is not a lot of sound work on the effectiveness of psychological interventions with sex offenders. Some researchers claim that research on treatment programmes does not show that they are effective in reducing reoffending or in changing attitudes and behaviour and, as this is the case, they should not be used. The argument is that you would not use a drug which had not been tested properly to treat a physical illness so why should you use a psychological treatment which has not been shown to work effectively to change behaviour or cognition? On the other hand, some researchers claim that psychological treatments for sex offenders do work. One study (Alexander, 1999), which looked at all of the available research on treatment programmes (seventy-nine studies involving almost 11,000 offenders) showed that people who participated in relapse prevention programmes had a 7.2 per cent re-arrest rate compared with 17.6 per cent for untreated offenders. These data suggest that offenders must be treated because there is a chance of changing behaviour and stopping abuse. One of the problems with looking at the effectiveness of programmes is what outcome measure to use. Many evaluations use reoffending rates as a measure, but this is problematic when trying to look at the effects of treatments on young offenders, many of whom are treated outside the criminal justice system. Researchers also suggest that, given the low reported reconviction rates for sex offenders (between twenty and three per cent compared to over sixty per cent for burglars), reconviction data are not statistically sensitive enough to pick up the positive effects of treatment and that psychometric test scores should be used more often.

management of offenders

It is clear that the public are protected from sexual offenders while they are in prison, but how does the criminal justice system protect the public either once offenders are released or while they are being punished in the community? When sex offenders are released, they have a licence which they have to keep to. This might mean that they have to live at a particular address or to observe a curfew which is enforced with an electronic tag. They also may be prohibited from entering certain localities or making contact with certain individuals or groups of people (especially victims), and may have restrictions on types of employment. Failure to comply with these standards could result in an offender being returned to custody.

Recent laws in the UK have shown a move toward consideration of victim and public safety, with the phrase 'public protection' used and acted on much more widely. Both the Sex Offenders Register and the development of Multi-Agency Public Protection Arrangements (MAPPAs) were developed to manage offenders who are considered to be at high risk of harming others within the community (sex offenders and those committed for serious violent acts).

The national Sex Offenders Register was set up after the passing of the Sex Offender Act 1997. The Act meant that offenders who had committed certain sexual offences had to lodge their details with the police. Since the Sexual Offences Act 2003, which came into force in May 2004, the requirements of registration have been tightened. Offenders have to notify the police of their details, including name, address and National Insurance number, within three days of leaving prison or moving home (previously this was fourteen days). The police may also take photographs of the offenders and their fingerprints. Offenders also have to tell police about any address they may stay at for more than seven days within a twelve-month period and have to annually re-confirm their details. One senior police officer stated that ninety-seven per cent of offenders who should be registered had done so. Offenders must also inform the police if they intend to travel abroad, and the new law has also introduced Foreign Travel Orders, which means that some offenders will not be allowed to travel abroad if there is evidence that the offenders intend to cause harm to children under sixteen in another country. This should help in reducing the impact to other countries of sex tourism, where offenders go with the intention of having sex with children.

In 2001 MAPPAs were set up to supervise violent, dangerous and sexual offenders within the community. The police and probation service will manage sex offenders if they are required to register with the police or have had a prison sentence of longer than a year. The arrangements are carried out by a Multi-Agency Public Protection Panel (MAPPP), which is made up of police, probation, social services, housing, health and youth offending teams. Since 2004 the MAPPPs must also have two lay people on the panels; these are people from the community in which the offender lives. The aim of the MAPPP is to increase public safety by reducing serious reoffending through making sure that the whereabouts and the behaviour of the offenders are supervised and managed. A police officer involved in the MAPPPs said recently that it was essential that people who were involved in managing this group of offenders had the right attitude to the work. The police officer was supporting one offender who had been reluctant to work with the police and had been difficult to deal with. The officer felt that he was making progress with the offender and he knew where the offender was and what he was doing. The police officer went on a regular visit to see the offender with a new colleague. During the visit the new colleague started to make negative remarks to the offender, saying that his behaviour was despicable, that he should not have been let out of prison, and that he did not deserve all the support and protection he was getting. The police officer was very unhappy about this and reported that they have not been able to meet the offender since. Poor management has meant that this offender, rather than being supervised and his risk of reoffending managed, has been driven underground, which is what the work of the MAPPP aims to avoid.

One of the problem areas is how to help people who think that they are having inappropriate thoughts and are worried about their behaviour. There are very few places that people can go to get support and treatment before they come to the attention of the police. In recent years, though, an organization called Stop it Now! has been set up in the UK and Ireland, based on an American model, to help change this situation.

Criminal psychology helps our understanding of the nature of sex offending in many ways. It helps us understand the impact of poor parenting on behaviour and see how abuse in childhood may have an impact on adult behaviour. It also shows how adult behaviour, when coupled with childhood experiences, may affect people's offending. Models of offending behaviour can be developed from our understanding of psychological make up, which can then be used to help create treatment programmes. The

STOP IT NOW!

'Stop it Now! UK and Ireland' is a campaign which aims to help stop child abuse and to protect children. It supports multi-agency projects (this includes organizations which work with children such as the police, social services, health and voluntary organizations) and tries to raise awareness of the nature of abuse, change attitudes towards abuse so that people are more willing to talk about it, and change the behaviour of abusers and potential abusers.

The campaign is aimed at adults who have abused or are thinking about abusing. The campaign will offer support and advice for potential offenders and to help them change their behaviour. This is one of the first organizations in the UK which will help people who have not yet come to the attention of public agencies. It helps the families and friends of abusers to recognize the signs of abuse and offer advice about the support available. It also seeks to help parents in recognizing the signs of abuse in their children. It offers a telephone help line, runs media campaigns, sends out information leaflets, holds public meetings and trains professionals in the prevention of abuse.

www.stopitnow.org.uk

research skills of criminal psychologists are also used in evaluating the effectiveness of treatment, which can then feed into improvements in treatment for dangerous and sexual offenders. The work of criminal psychologists helps government, policy-makers and practitioners to improve treatment, management and supervision of offenders, which increases public protection and safety.

recommended further reading

Alexander, M. A. (1999) Sex offender treatment efficacy revisited. *Sexual Abuse: A Journal of Research and Treatment*, 11, 101–16.

Cobley, C. (2000) *Sex offenders: Law, policy and practice.* Bristol: Jordans.

Marshall, W. L., Anderson, D. and Fernandez, Y. M. (1999). *Cognitive behavioural treatment of sex offenders.* Chichester: Wiley.

Nicholas, S., Povey, D., Walker, A. and Kershaw, C. (2005) *Crime in England and Wales, 2004/2005: Home Office Statistical Bulletin.* Available at http://www.homeoffice.gov.uk/rds/pdfs05/hosb1105.pdf.

Ryan, G. and Lane, S. (1997) *Juvenile sexual offending: Causes consequences and corrections,* 2nd edn. San Francisco, CA: Jossey-Bass.

Hanson, R. K. (1997) Invoking sympathy – Assessment and treatment of empathy deficits among sexual offenders. In B. Schwartz and H. Cellini *The sex offender: New insights, treatment innovations and legal developments.* New Jersey: Civic Research Institute.

Thomas, T. (2005) *Sex crime: Sex offending and society,* 2nd edn. Cullumpton, UK: Willan Publishing.

Youth Justice Board (2004) *Youth Justice Annual Statistics, 2003/2004.* Available at http://www.youth-justice-board.gov.uk/Publications/Scripts/prodView.asp?idproduct=199andeP=YJB.

index

Note to Index: *cr. ps.* is criminal psychologist